The Eagle's Nest

THE IMMIGRANT SERIES, BOOK 1

Mary Barton

Copyright © 2015 Mary Barton
All rights reserved.
ISBN: 1519183925
ISBN-13: 9781519183927

Cover art by Alkestida/www.shutterstock.com.
Edited by Gail R. Bergan, www.bergan.com.

Table of Contents

Acknowledgments	v
One Door Closes	1
An Answered Prayer	10
Hope Ignited	18
Loss of Faith	24
United Dreams	29
Escape	33
The Journey	37
New Beginnings	42
Through the Gauntlet	46
Diverted	49
New Territory	53
Indoctrination	57
Strike	60
Brotherly Love	66
Challenges	70
Winter's Gift	74
Disaster	79
Recovery	83
Learning the Land	87
Introductions	93
Engaging the Enemy	98
Saying Goodbye	103
Reuniting	107
Divine Intervention	111
Wonders Abound	116
The Hand of God	120

Treasures Found	124
Visions Revealed	128
Commuting	131
The Neighbors	135
Renewed Hope	140
Blessed Unions	146
Paradise Found	150
Glossary	155

Acknowledgments

A work of historical fiction is the result of many people doing what they do best: living, loving and pursuing their dreams. This book is a story based on the documented facts, and family memories, of my pioneer ancestors and the time period in which they lived. Where facts were not available, logically deducted fiction was used to fill in their story.

I would like to express my sincere gratitude to all the writers, researchers, journalists, and chronologists whose work added to the authenticity of this labor of love. In particular, I would like to thank the many men and women who had the foresight to publish the histories of the original pioneers of Walsh County, North Dakota in four volumes of *Walsh Heritage: A Story of Walsh County and Its Pioneers*. I am deeply indebted to the members of The Walsh County Historical Society, who gathered the histories from hundreds of families that civilized the plains of North Dakota.

I am also particularly grateful to the authors of *The Polish Peasant in Europe and America*, who studied and chronicled the Polish emigrants who chose America as their home. Their provided insight into the Polish character and history was invaluable to the completion of this story.

If not for the strength and determination the pioneers used to endure the challenges of the wild frontier, to seek a better world in which to live and raise their children, America would be an entirely different world.

One Door Closes

"The gown must be ready in time for the funeral," Manya Riske insisted in her anxiety as she paced the tiny, dirt floored cottage. Manya had barely been able to keep still for the measurements. There was so much to do. Nor, she had to admit, was she accustomed to giving orders. Piotor had always managed their affairs, as was proper, even from his sickbed. Strong, sensible, reliable Piotor was always in control. *But now all that must change,* she thought distractedly. She had three children and soon a grandchild to provide for, and yet how she was to accomplish that was still a mystery. She felt both bereft and scattered since her husband Piotor had died. Her heart felt as heavy as a boulder but her mind leaped like a bullfrog from one responsibility to another that somehow must be accomplished before their final farewell.

All she truthfully wanted to do was lie down and weep, she thought, as her downcast eyes took in the faded, threadbare gown that had served her meager needs for the past few years. Scandalized by what she saw, her determination rose. They were not rich but they were *gospodarz* now, as her son Jan had reminded her, and they had a landowner's reputation to uphold. She wouldn't allow her husband's memory to be tarnished by not appearing in proper mourning clothes. Although he habitually thought of the welfare of others, Jan had surprised her with his insistence that he bring the seamstress to the family farm this morning. *He is such a blessing,* Manya surmised, *and had grown into a fine young man.* Perhaps somehow together the family would manage to meet their obligations, despite the unrest once again building in the country.

"What would people think if I appeared in this?" she demanded of the seamstress, as she straightened her stout, middle-aged shoulders, defending her request. Zofia glanced at her in surprise. "Jan insists his father be well-represented. Elizbieta will fit into my old gown, and Marta is young enough to manage with her Sunday-best covered with my black shawl."

Manya gasped at her uncharacteristic harshness toward her old friend. Recognizing her unintentional rudeness, "Forgive me," she said softly, as her errant emotions surfaced yet again reminding her of the unspeakable, that her wise, loving Piotor was truly gone. Barely restraining her grief with a sob, she continued rapidly, "*Oj*, what am I going to do without him? He fought so hard for Poland only to have it end like this!"

Manya stopped abruptly as she realized the admission she had just announced in her anguish. *God forgive her, what had she done?* She shot a quick glance at Zofia to assess the reaction to her statement.

No one knew of Piotor's involvement in the January Uprising against Russia in what seemed like yesterday but felt like ages reckoned by the pain he and his countrymen had endured since then. Everyone thought his shattered leg and the brace he had been forced to wear had been the result of an accident on the farm. It was still dangerous to admit compliance with the rebels—so many had died or disappeared into the Siberian wastelands during those harsh times. Only a select few knew that he had helped Count Zamenski in Poland's bid for freedom. *Even friends could turn against you*, Manya thought nervously.

"Of course," the seamstress agreed quickly, ignoring Manya's revelation as she set the measurements she had scribbled beside the sample of black fabric for the gown. "God willing, the dress will be ready on time, Manya," she assured her.

Zofia's heart went out to the newly bereft woman. It was so difficult to become a widow, as she knew, *God rest her husband's soul*. She had worn her own mourning apparel for several years now, with no suitor in sight with so many good men laid to rest before their time. But as there were few real secrets in their small Polish community, Manya's disclosure didn't surprise her. "It must have been such a shock for you when it happened," Zofia commented trying to calm Mrs. Riske's misgivings, as she glanced across to the small storage room within which she knew Piotor's corpse lay awaiting burial. She had shown her respects when she arrived but now Elizbieta, Manya's oldest daughter, knelt and prayed beside the body placed on planks between two chairs beneath holy pictures framed in polished wood, the Easter palm, and an herb bouquet blessed on Assumption Day.

Manya visibly relaxed and wearily sank onto the worn rough-hewn wood bench beside the cottage's equally worn table. "I never knew the Almighty Lord could take life so quickly," she confessed. "Piotor was still weak from his fever and cough but thought he felt well enough to get up on his own. When I returned from soaking the laundry and saw him swaying beside the hearth, I scolded him for being out of bed. He admitted that he was feeling winded so I helped him lie back down. Once he was settled, he suggested I make myself a cup of tea while he rested. So I did."

She clutched her embroidered handkerchief in her hands. "A few minutes later when our dog Duke began howling, I shooed him outdoors and checked on Piotor. His lips were blue...." She stopped speaking in order to gain control of her emotions. "I immediately opened the doors and windows so his soul could fly free into eternity, of course, and covered the mirror and stopped the clock. Then I prepared his body myself," she admitted shamefacedly. It was customary to hire a death-preparer to do those duties, but the Riskes couldn't afford this, so she had carried out the cleansing and clothing process herself determined that only she, after 30 years of marriage, would touch her beloved husband's body. "The doctor said it was the lung sickness that took him so quickly. I will miss him so! Praise God that Father Ignacio had visited him the day before to hear his confession and give him the Holy Sacrament."

"Of course you will. We all will," Zofia assured her, squeezing Manya's shoulder gently. "Bless Father Ignacio," she continued as she began placing her supplies in her basket. "He is always there when someone needs him even though he must do it surreptitiously. He has always fought for the souls of the people and the welfare of the Fatherland, no matter what the Russians decree. It is such a sacrilege that they closed so many of the convents and churches! But Piotor is surely beside our Heavenly Father, Manya. He was such a good man. Your dog knew he had passed, too. Animals always do," she added knowingly.

Manya nodded in agreement. She then roused enough to remember her manners, that in a Polish household, a guest in the house was God in the house. "Would you like a cup of tea, Zofia?" she offered as she rose from her seat.

Zofia shook her head, pulling her shawl around her shoulders. "No, bless you, Manya, I must begin immediately on the gown. I will send word when it is ready." Zofia emitted a sigh herself. She wished the order had been for three dresses. The one gown was the only work she had found in weeks, business was so bad. But she had managed to get by in other ways, she thought as she murmured the expected, "Go with God, Manya."

Manya nodded, returning the brief hug, ready once again to continue chiseling at her list of duties to accomplish within the mandatory three-day burial period. "Jan will take you back, Zofia. Thank you for taking the time to save me a trip into town. May God bless you, my dear."

Jan drove Zofia quickly back to her cottage, then began posting *klepsydra* on the church doors and outside public houses throughout the village. He personally delivered the death notices to their relatives, with promises from them that they would notify the more distant family members. The notice was a simple one, symbolizing the passage of time with its ultimate result:

> "In deep bereavement we wish to inform that on October 8, 1869, the late lamented Piotor Riske, an active member of All Saints Church and a former laborer for Count Zamenski, died at the age of 52. A brief funeral ceremony and *pogrzeb* will be held at the family farm on Drobna Road, five miles south of the village center on October 12, 1869 at noon. A belated *Requiem* mass will be held in his honor during normal Sunday services at All Saints Church. This information has been provided by the deeply bereaved wife Manya, daughter Elizbieta, son Jan, daughter Marta, and son-in-law Chester Waska."

It wasn't right, Jan knew and deeply regretted that his father wouldn't be buried at the church cemetery—but they had no choice. They could not afford neither a plot nor a stone. His father's doctor bills had been unrelentingly high and the poor harvest hadn't left enough for such luxuries. He knew the family would barely make it through the winter. Saddened by conditions that were beyond his control, he quickly finished his tasks and hurried home to complete funeral preparations.

❊

Jan went to the window at the sound of a carriage pulling into the stone-rimmed farmyard. Word had traveled quickly about Piotor Riske's passing. In the past three days, the ancient *chata* had roiled with activity in preparation for today's funeral.

Piotor's remains had been dressed in his threadbare suit and placed in a simple coffin constructed by Jan's brother-in-law Chester, awaiting internment after the customary round-the-clock mourners said their prayers and heartfelt goodbyes to the candle-surrounded corpse. A grave had been dug beneath the lone oak tree on the property using pick-axes and heated water to penetrate the nearly frozen ground.

Jan and his two sisters had severed the heads from a variety of precious fowl whose aroma now wafted from the large stucco-faced brick oven. Extra rye bread and angel's wings were cooling on two overhead beams that spanned the chata's open living space. Jan's older sister Elizbieta tended clay pots bubbling on the open hearth to feed those who would gather to give strength to the Riske family.

As Jan stepped to the door checking once again that his black armband was in place, the sounds of clicking beads and guttering candles emerged from the room where his mother took her turn silently praying the rosary to help direct her husband's soul to heaven. Candlelight and shadows danced a ghoulish duet off the corpse's ashen features, making his body seem filled with life where there was none.

A small willow basket near the door, beneath the holy water font, overflowed with scapulars and saint embellished holy cards from those who had known his beloved *ojciec*. Jan was gratified for the Catholic masses that had been purchased and the candles lit for the soul of his father. Even their former landlord's wife, Countess Zamenski, instructed her estate foreman to deliver sausage, cheese, brown bread, and vodka in remembrance of their long association.

Despite the goodwill demonstrated by their friends, generally high-spirited and good-natured Jan was deeply disturbed by the sudden turn events had taken. Although he was aware that man never knew the time of his passing, in his anguish Jan wondered why God hadn't allowed his father to enjoy his freedom longer. They had been released from the yoke of dominion for such a short period!

Serfdoms had been abolished to placate the peasants and punish the nobility under Russian rule after the January Uprising by the Polish nobility in 1864. For the past five years the former Riske serfs no longer toiled on Count Zamenski's land but worked their own allotted twenty *morgs*. They were no longer owned by the nobility, to be beaten by foremen for any trifle or tossed from their homes for not fulfilling six days a week of forced labor on the manor estate. Such a miracle it had been! In their exuberance, the former virtual slaves had liberally passed the glasses filled from their stills hidden deep within the forests.

The Riskes and their friends had rejoiced in their independence as landowners. They were thrilled to finally be able to sow and reap their own land during daylight hours, and not deplete their energies on Count Zamenski's estate. Some prospered and others failed under the new godsend. But after three short years of respite from the whip, the Devil had intervened and another ruthless ruler had replaced the Polish nobility in running their lives.

In 1867 parts of Poland, including the small village between Poznan and Warsaw where the 'Riskes lived, had formally been placed under the dominion of the Russian Empire. Tempers flared, then turned to despair, at the new restrictions and escalating taxations. The subjugation of the Polish people by Czar Alexander II was barely tolerable, with the Polish language forbidden to be spoken in public or in any schools, and prohibitions on any Polish gatherings since rumors of war were on the rise again.

Despite the many regulations placed upon them, Piotor had taught his children to be devout Roman Catholics, and to have faith and trust in the Almighty Father. Until his final day he fully believed that someday Poland would be free again. Jan's confidence in that hope had died with his father as his bitterness simultaneously increased toward the Russians.

Jan himself had dragged his father from further injury by Russian sabers during the skirmish for independence. There had been no repercussions due to Jan's swift actions to remove his wounded father from beneath the hooves of Russian horses and hide him in a church. They had stayed there until he could be transported safely home with the help of Father Ignacio as he traveled his visitation route to the smaller villages. But memories were long and Jan never forgot who was responsible.

Jan had watched helplessly as his father's wounds failed to heal properly. Although he and his two sisters had compensated for their father's subsequent lack of strength and worked their land with a vengeance to spare their father's health, Piotor had finally succumbed to his weakened state. The Riske blood was a part of their land, but soon, to his family's grief, the ground would embrace his beloved remains.

Jan opened the door with the inscription K+M+B (the initials of Kaspar, Melchior, and Balthazar, the Three Kings from Epiphany Day) over the doorway to see his father's elder sister, Patrika, and her husband, Alexandre, standing with a towel-wrapped dish in her hands as Chester and his cousin Josef unhitched their horse. Stepping in quickly from the early October weather, she handed her nephew the bundle.

"Oj, my poor orphan. Such terrible times these are. Here is a little *pierogi* in honor of your father, my dear. Piotor always did love my dumplings," she said with a sigh.

Jan took the dish from her and gave a slight bow, "How kind of you, Aunt Patrika. Welcome, Uncle Alexandre, please come in. Matka is in with ojciec now."

"Then we will go in to her," she replied as she removed her gloves. Patrika placed her coat on a bench near the door and reached up to untie her babushka as Uncle Alexandre removed his hat and coat. Patrika knew the Riskes couldn't hold a traditional funeral for her brother, *shameful as it was*, she thought, automatically making the sign of the cross using the church-blessed holy water beside the door. But neither could they afford to be dragged off to prison by the Cossacks if they did. *How her brother would find his way to paradise without a funeral procession was unfathomable. These were such trying times.*

Life had been particularly unkind to her patriotic brother, although it was no more generous to the rest of their Kashubian relatives. They had just traveled 25 miles from Prussian German-occupied Poland where conditions were little better than in Russian-occupied Poland. Each nationality was trying their hardest to rid the Poles of their heritage. First the Prussian Germans, then the Russians fought for possession of their beleaguered country. *Praise the Almighty Father*, her other brother and his family had chosen to leave Poland to get away from all the turmoil. Although she missed them these past years, he was a generous man, and had endured bereavement himself with the loss of his first wife. She knew he would be saddened to learn of his brother's passing.

Patrika embraced her nephew's sturdy frame, and whispered, "I have something that may brighten your heart." She withdrew a letter from her reticule and gave it to him, "Look at it later when things are more settled. Uncle Martin sent it to you enclosed with one for me." Jan nodded his head and placed the letter from his father's brother into the basket by the door as he turned to set the dish on the kitchen table.

"Elizbieta and Marta, come and give your old aunt a hug," Patrika declared as she glanced about the neat but crowded room. Sixteen-year-old Marta jumped down from her oven berth where she had been warming her bones after tending to her chores. Elizbieta, her protruding belly evident beneath her apron, set down her wooden spoon and swiftly came forward to greet her aunt.

Patrika and Alexandre were the first of many visitors that day calling to kiss the cold hand of a patriot who had fought unsuccessfully for Polish independence. They arrived surreptitiously, one by one, to avoid notice of village officials. Although it was illegal to gather in groups, no one could stop these "stubborn as a *Kaszub*" Poles from paying their respects to an old friend.

At noon the Riskes stood beside Father Ignacio as he intoned the last rites over the coffin that had been properly tapped on the doorsill in farewell as it was carried out of their home. The mourners ringed the grave beneath the ancient oak which stretched its barren limbs to the heavens where Piotor would be kept alive in the Riske thoughts as they went about the process of living.

Father Ignacio addressed the gathering, reminding the mourners of Piotor's well-led life, and the blessings he had received in the form of his family and friends through his continued support and observance of church doctrine. "Eternal rest grant unto him, oh Lord," he canted, and the mourners responded in unison, "And let the perpetual Light shine upon him."

The priest blessed the coffin with holy water and threw a handful of soil on it, saying: "From dust you came and to dust you shall return, but the Lord will raise you on the last day. Live in peace. Amen."

Manya looked red-eyed but composed by the gravesite as if the new gown she wore had given her strength to endure this tragedy. As he stood beside her, Jan gazed over the black-attired assembly of brave comrades, each bearing lit candles, who had gathered in his father's memory. He blew out his own candle and tossed his handful of dirt on the lid of the coffin, silently vowing one day to replace the wooden cross at the head of the grave with a marble stone. An unheard, heart-wrenching farewell elicited from the depths of his soul to the father he had so admired and loved, then he murmured the all too familiar litany, "Dust to dust. God's will be done."

Solemn, weeping, and tear-stained guests followed his lead until the opening of the grave was filled quickly with the remaining dirt. Then the attending black beribboned children, with the younger ones firmly guided by the elder, placed bouquets of dried flowers, autumn leaves, ferns and pine cones on the leveled ground, replacing the bleakness of death with the illusion of beauty. With the unenviable deed finally accomplished, Jan turned resolutely in the direction of the farmhouse for the *stypa*.

Now they would console and cheer each other with good food and fond memories, and toast the deceased, as was the Polish way, with a little vodka. Although the Riskes were not overly friends-of-the-glass, they would respect Polish custom in honor of their father. That night Jan drank deeply to alleviate his grief.

An Answered Prayer

Jan stood in the brisk morning air staring at the dusting of snow that cloaked each tree branch and blade of grass in the surrounding countryside. It had been a glorious snowfall, the remnants of which sparkled like polished gemstones in the bright sunlight, which Jan had thoroughly relished while walking his forbidden trap line. Poaching game was a necessity of life many of the poor had become adept at during the aftermath of war and was an aspect of survival he continued during the current unrest to add to his family's cellar. Jan firmly believed animals of the streams and forests were given by God to any man who needed them and had the skill to harvest them. They were gifts from God just as surely as the snowfall had been, regardless of manmade boundaries and land titles.

Jan had always enjoyed wintertime, and despite his father's death, this winter was no exception. He looked forward to this season to renew his spirits, give birth to his plans and seek inward to hear God's path for him.

The silence now surrounding him reminded Jan of when, as a little boy, his father had said that God made the world quiet when it snowed so that man could hear His will. Ever since then, Jan had made it a habit to listen for God's message whenever it snowed, although this time he believed he had already received it.

Jan had decided he was going to do it. God, in the guise of Kasper Koswalski, an old friend of the family, had convinced him. Kasper, who as a horse trader traveled freely about the country, told Jan that Russian Cossack patrols were dragging Polish youth off the streets conscripting them into military service. With the suspicions about his father's loyalties and their association with Count Zamenski, it was no longer safe for him in Poland. Jan knew he would be dead or imprisoned within months if he was caught because, God forgive him, he could not disguise his hatred of the Russians.

Jan didn't want to join military service, forcibly or willingly. At twenty-two, he had seen all of the hangings, revolutionary bloodshed, and aftermath of destruction he wanted to in his young life. He had witnessed the Russian attempts in 1863 to erase Polish nationality and to thwart Polish independence with military skirmishes between 10,000 "knife-and-fork" equipped Polish revolutionists against 30,000 hardened Russian troops.

He remembered the terror of the fires and the slaughters of 1864. He couldn't, wouldn't, waste seven to fifteen years of his life in the Russian military assigned to the harsh Siberian wastelands of the Russian regime. He knew his beloved Poland, in fact, no longer existed. It had been summarily annexed by and divided between Russia, Prussian Germany, and Austria. He had pondered long and hard about his future and that of his country, and now he was about to trust in the Almighty and change his destiny.

Jan had ruthlessly inspected his options, his desires and his skills since that conversation, and in his humble opinion, he felt he could succeed. He *must* succeed to help not only himself but his family survive. Although not highly book educated, he could read, was fluent in both German and Polish, with a smattering of Russian, and believed he knew enough to get by.

Growing up in the 1840s, learning to read was not only unnecessary and unproductive for most serfs, it was scorned by the downtrodden community itself as putting on airs. Jan knew he would never be a scholar, nor did he want to be. He had God, the Ten Commandments and the priests to guide him, and that was enough for him. But Father Ignacio believed that learning to read was essential for the serfs in this changing world and Piotor had insisted his children learn in secret, despite the derision they endured when their neighbors discovered.

Learning to read had not magically altered their fate, but it had made them more aware of the changes and opportunities currently available to them. The ability to read had given the Riskes knowledge they could rely on, rather than the rumor and gossip by which most serfs lived. Reading the *Przeglad Polski* (Polish Review), or the *Gazeta Narodowa* (National Gazette), when he could get his hands on them, had given Jan information about the world he lived in and the forces that could govern his fate.

Jan knew his primary talents consisted in his ability to hunt, trap and farm. He loved working the land and was well-equipped to do so. Although not tall at 173 cm, his stocky body rippled with strength and the limits to his endurance had yet to be found. He was an expert at animal husbandry, and had an inexplicable affinity with the magical dance of nature. The thriving plants, seeking out new avenues of growth, spoke to him of the necessity for boldness in life and equally demonstrated the benefits of seeking fertile ground to fulfill his potential. He had traveled with the harvest teams into Prussian Germany since their independence from slavery and knew life thrived in divergent venues. While many boys dreamed of being soldiers, Jan preferred the less revered role of farmer. It was nurturing life and nourishing a family that made the man, not wantonly dealing death to life's fellow sojourners.

After glancing about once more to make sure he was alone, Jan reached down to release the stiff body of the marten from his handmade snare. He thanked the soft, dark-brown specimen for its sacrifice, as he simultaneously thanked God for this gift. While placing the luxuriantly furred body into his sack, Jan whimsically wished he could receive a small sign of God's approval of his plans. *Forgive me, blessed Father,* he mentally chided himself for his lack of faith, but he knew it was a drastic step he was planning to take. *Surely freedom is not too great a boon to ask.* As he reset the trap, ever vigilant to his surroundings as had been drummed into him in these perilous times, a movement to his right captured Jan's attention.

Unperturbed by the whiteness now sheltering the land, a magnificent eagle lifted from its nest, spread its black wings and floated in circles directly overhead, then soared west toward the lake to begin its daily hunt. Jan watched in awe, and gratitude, as the symbol of Poland pointed the way he was to go. Jan knew the eagle would use his God-given gifts to harvest the bounty provided him. *Praise God,* Jan thought, as he recognized the hallowed sign God had sent him. He quickly made the sign of the cross and began the trek back to the farmhouse to await Josef.

"The dogs almost got me this time!" Josef exclaimed as he scraped the door over the packed snow into the Riske household a short time later. "I just managed to escape by hiding in the manor woods. I'm sorry I'm late. I got your message. What did you want to see me about?"

Jan cast a worried look at Josef as his younger cousin threw off his patched, hand-me-down jacket. "The honorable Viceroy, Count Friedrich Wilhelm Rembert von Berg, is allowing them to become more bold," he said as he threw his arm around his favorite cousin and guided him to a seat. "I didn't attend mass since the patrols have begun grabbing the faithful outside of church on Sundays. Soon the curs will be going house to house. That is what we must discuss. I have something to show you."

While going through the willow basket of mourning cards to take one to church with her last week, Marta had discovered the letter addressed to Jan that their aunt had given him when she attended Piotor's funeral. Jan had forgotten about it in his grief but had read it many times since then and now held it firmly in his hands. "Listen to this," he said guardedly. "It's from Uncle Martin."

He read:

"My dearest nephew Jan,

Blessed be Jesus Christus! And I hope that you will answer for centuries and centuries. Amen.

I send low bows and good wishes to you brother Piotor, your lovely wife Manya, my beautiful nieces Elizbieta and Marta, and you, good Chester. How are you succeeding? We are here alone, like orphans or stones in a field, without you, our family beside us. But we have been successful. America is so vast and bountiful! Our family is proceeding well. Praise God, we live better than a lord in Poland!

But in America, in a small town, a Pole is as solitary as an island. Why don't you consider immigrating? There are so many opportunities here! There is homestead land that is said to be as fertile as the Garden of Eden in Dakota Territory—for free!

The newspapers report that Chancellor Bismarck is pushing for unification of Germany and that Russia is preparing to go to war again. Why do you stay in such misery when there is 160 acres of abundant earth here for the taking?

You must just live on the property for five years, not be away from it for more than six months each year, cultivate it and it is yours. The land is available to the head of a family or anyone who is 21 years old. The soil is rich and overflowing with game, fish and fowl. The fur trade alone can make you rich. My sons Julius and Frank are ready to claim this land. Come here to this heaven-on-earth and we can build a Polish community of our own.

In America the War Between the States is over, God rest my son Auguste's soul, but the slaves are free and peace treaties have placed the Indians on reservations. There is no fear of bloodshed here! I will send you money for ship-tickets and you can pay me back later from your earnings.

Here is a newspaper article about the Dakota Territory with a map showing this new land. If you leave in the spring you can plant your first crops together. Think on this. We would love to have you here with us.

We send embraces and kisses to all of you.

May God make you happy and keep you safe.

Your Uncle Martin

General Delivery

Winona, Minnesota, America"

The enclosed newspaper clipping was annotated in Polish and described the "Myth of Dakota Territory." The article extolled the abundance of available land and the fruits of labor to be had through hard work. It described the virtues of the land and how good and just people could realize the American Dream of home ownership. It had convinced Jan that God had answered his prayers.

"What do you think?" Jan asked quickly, hoping his cousin would see the merit in emigrating.

"Dog's blood! America!" Josef murmured. He looked at the map attached to the newspaper article. Dakota Territory was a vast region in the middle of the North American continent. In the years since their Uncle had emigrated, Josef and Jan had devoured all of the news from Uncle Martin first doubting, then envying, his prosperity. Before now, neither he nor Jan had the means, or incentive, to consider emigrating. Now with the offer of help from their uncle and the very real possibility of their loss of freedom to the Russian regime, he leaned back closer to the warm hearth and considered the idea.

Josef was the third son of landless peasants forced to send their children into service to make ends meet. Beginning in his eleventh year, the tall, brawny youth had been a stablehand for a local lord, grooming and learning to train horses for service. He had bunked in the barn, had meals and clothes provided along with a meager wage he properly gave to his family to help feed his younger brothers and sisters. For the past two years after the lord's lands were confiscated by the Russians, Josef had worked in the coal mines of the central plains.

"160 acres for free!" Jan exclaimed. "Just think of it. It would take us the rest of our lives, if we even could, to buy that here. In five years it could be ours for just a little hard work. I think it is something we should seriously consider. I want to go and hope you will go with me. You know Martin. He has lived there for more than ten years and owns his own farm! Our cousins Julius and Frank are about our age and eager to take advantage of the opportunity. There is nothing here but death or drudgery for us! I am tired of this life, Josef! Chester and Elizbieta, and mother and Marta can work this property. You have nothing. What do you have to lose?"

Jan unconsciously massaged his forehead as if to bring clarity to his arguments. "With Uncle Martin's offer our ship fees would be paid so all we would have to do is earn enough to get to the pier as well as traveling expenses. Since the land is free, we would need food and operating cash while we get the farms started. At the very least, there is much more work in America than there is here. You could earn enough there to raise your own horses on your homestead!"

Josef's heart raced at that idea. That would be a miracle indeed! How he would love to establish his own stable! His work with the horses had been the happiest time of his life. Yes, the foreman had been a brute, slinging his whip at the slightest hint of laziness or poorly done work, but the animals had been magnificent. *Was this his chance to achieve that dream?* He knew it might be possible. Look at what Martin had accomplished since he had been in America, and here was newspaper proof that the offer was true.

"If Suzanna agrees to marry me," Jan continued as his face turned bright red in hopeful embarrassment, "she could cook for us while we break the soil and plant our crops. I know mother will object so soon after father's death, but I want to start a family before my juices run dry. My being gone won't be a burden to her if I send money to help them here. I've been figuring out what it will take and what we will need to get there. Say you will join me Josef," he pleaded.

Josef looked at his cousin thoughtfully. Both Jan and his older sister Elizbieta had been forced to postpone any thought of marriage while they were still under the rule of Count Zamenski, who must approve any wedding by his serfs. The uprisings in their country, helping their father on the farm after his "accident," adjusting to life as landowners, and making a small profit on their property had forced them both to remain single well past marriageable age.

Elizbieta at 25 years old had recently married and was about to bring forth her first child. She and her husband Chester shared one of the two handmade feather beds, with feathers painstakingly saved from their fowl over the years, and helped work the fields since their marriage. Jan's younger sister had moved from her floor berth behind the oven and now shared the other bed in the crowded cottage with his Aunt Manya since Piotor's death. Marta did her part in maintaining the farm by pasturing the Riske's small flock of geese and gathering wood for the fire. Although their cellar was currently filled with potatoes, rutabagas, and several barrels of sauerkraut, Josef had endured the pangs of hunger and agreed with Jan that 20 morgs of land could not support three families.

Neither he nor Jan could prosper here. With the Polish nobility dethroned, work for wages was more difficult than ever to find, unless you hired out to the Germans who forced you to break God's laws to eat meat on Friday and work on Sunday. No extra money, or land, was available to allow them to begin their own families.

Josef liked Suzanna and got along well with her. He knew Jan had been courting her before his uncle's demise. Although he had no woman of his own who he would leave broken-hearted if he left, he knew he would find the right woman when the time came. Right now, just staying alive was hardship enough and today's escape from capture had been entirely too close. He held no place in his heart for living under Russian boots and the thought of traveling to the new land held great appeal. If he saved his wages until they sailed, he might have enough to cover his expenses. Although he held no fascination for traveling over the wide ocean, preferring a fine horse to take him where he wanted to go, he knew he could endure the voyage for such unbelievable riches. He grinned at his cousin and replied, "With God's help, let's do it."

Both men jumped to their feet in their exuberance and clasped together in a bear hug to seal their agreement, then immediately began to discuss what needed to be done. Father Ignacio had helped Martin make the necessary arrangements when he immigrated to America. They would speak to him first. Only when their plans were firmly in place would they ask for the blessings of their and Suzanna's parents.

Hope Ignited

Suzanna glanced anxiously out the window from her perch by the large kitchen table. She had boiled water for tea, fed her brothers and sisters buckwheat porridge for breakfast after their required fast prior to mass, and arranged a platter of pastries as her mother had requested. While her siblings noisily played a card game on the cleared table, she sat stiffly upright, her hands clenched tightly in her lap with thumbs firmly touching for luck.

Jan and Chester had asked to speak to her mother and father with Father Ignacio after church services. They had sent her and her siblings home in the wagon almost two hours ago. Helen and Stephani Wojek were old friends of Jan's parents. As former Count Zamenski serfs, they had known each other from childhood, as did their children. Jan had helped the Wojeks bring in the harvest many times, and now her fate rested in their hands. There could only be one reason Jan and Chester wanted to speak to her parents privately—but why was it taking so long?

Suzanna and her family had attended Elizbieta and Chester's wedding just last year. Since the heartless Russians forbade Catholic churches to conduct matrimonial services in church anymore, Father Ignacio had consented to hold a secret ceremony on the Riske property after the civil one.

When Suzanna had caught Elizbieta's tossed wedding veil, Jan had teased her relentlessly about being the next to wed and began taking advantage of every opportunity to see her. He had sought her out after the midnight Solemn High Mass on star-evening and shared a forbidden portion of his Christmas wafer with her. He had presented her with a huge red batik Easter goose egg etched especially for her and he had brought her precious hog bristles for fixing shoes. After planting began in the spring, he would rush through his chores so he could visit with her and her family. Suzanna had behaved completely appropriately as befit any young maiden, of course, but had finally discovered she had fallen in love with the rakish ball of energy.

She loved the way Jan was a true Pole, always optimistic with a ready laugh despite the responsibilities laid upon his shoulders. He was grudgingly admired for his immense energy and determination. A man of faith, he was ambitious, adventurous and before his father's sudden passing, had indicated he was eager to start a life with her. But with his father gone, would they be allowed to marry? It was considered disrespectful, and bad luck, to marry so soon after a death in the family.

But these are modern times, she thought, tossing her long blond braid over her shoulder. Surely her parents wouldn't deny their union. Praise God, if they did give their approval, she would not be unhappy at their decision.

Suzanna's thoughts were interrupted as the Riske farm wagon rattled into the yard with her parents in tow. She watched as they descended from the wagon and saw her mother Helen hurry toward their cottage. Although the Wojek's had managed to build a small bedroom addition onto their one-room farmhouse to bed their growing family, the main room of the house was a mirror image of the Riske's.

"Suzanna, please set out the jugs," Suzanna's *matka* said with a bright smile. "Children, I want you to go outside and play for a while. We must talk to Suzanna alone for a few minutes. Is the water hot for tea?"

"*Tak*, matka," Suzanna replied, as the children hurried outdoors at their mother's request.

Helen observed the hope that lighted her daughter's lovely features as she nodded "yes" in answer to Suzanna's unasked question and gave her a quick hug. Helen knew her daughter would make any man a good wife and would be a mother as loving as the Blessed Virgin herself. Jan was a good man whom she loved as a son, but he was offering a more challenging life than one she may have chosen for Suzanna.

Although physically robust with all the strength that fresh air, vegetables and honest farm labor provided a body, Helen knew her daughter was at heart a timid woman, prone to avoid conflict and even the hint of adventure. She knew part of it was due to the wars they had endured, and the uncertainty caused by the brutality of their enemies, but part of it was her very nature. Susanna loved her home, family, country and its traditions. She relished the company and familiarity of her many aunts, uncles and cousins. With such a large family, one rarely needed to venture far for companionship. Helen knew it would take a strong woman to endure her future and somehow she must help Suzanna find the fortitude she would need in the days ahead. Pray God they had made the right decision.

"Compose yourself child," she said briefly, blinking back tears, "and remember that your father and I want only the best for you."

"Tak, matka," Suzanna immediately agreed, a delighted grin lighting her features. *I am to be married!* she thought as she set jugs on the table beside the wooden platter filled with poppy seed cake. As the men entered the room and settled themselves, Suzanna struggled to control her bubbling emotions and demurely poured tea into each of their mugs. Jan appeared uncharacteristically nervous but smiled hopefully at her as she and her mother took their seats.

"Jan has asked for your hand in marriage, Suzanna," her father began immediately, "and your mother and I have given our consent. He is a fine man and we will be proud to welcome him into our family."

Suzanna smiled radiantly at Jan, acknowledging her pleasure at the agreement. With a look of relief at her acceptance of him, he boldly reached his hand across the table to grasp hers.

"He plans to immigrate to America and take you there to build a life together," her father continued frankly.

Suzanna's rosy cheeks paled significantly as her startled eyes sought Jan's. *America!* Jan squeezed her hand tightly as hers went limp in his.

"Your mother and I believe his plans have merit, Suzanna. Jan is offering you the opportunity to have a large farm of your own in Dakota Territory and a more secure future in America. You will have the chance to raise children away from warfare. It is becoming much too dangerous here and you will be able to provide them with a more safe and abundant life there than here," he explained emphatically. "America is rich, and even if the crops fail, there is game and fish for the taking to sustain you. I know this is a surprise for you as Jan investigated the situation before speaking to us, or you, about his plans. But it is a well-conceived idea and he will make you a worthy husband. Mother, bring out the vodka so we can properly toast the betrothed couple."

Shocked but trying to hide her dismay, Suzanna quickly released Jan's hand as she stood to help her mother. After they drank to their health and were wished a 100 years of happiness and prosperity, Jan excitedly explained the details to her. Although the thought of free land was beyond anything she had ever imagined, her confidence was shaken to learn he was taking her to where savages lived and where there may not be civilized people for miles around. This was not what she had expected her married life to be!

Suzanna's tension was slightly alleviated when Jan explained that instead of posting the normal three-week bans before their wedding, he had received the blessing of Father Ignacio and his mother to marry prior to the end of the customary one year mourning period for his father. After an acceptable four-month waiting period to show respect for his passing, and due to the rising escalation of Russian military conscriptions, they would be married in February. Since it wasn't necessary to reach the frozen Dakota Territory until spring, she would have some time to come to terms with the many changes in her life—and they would have the opportunity to prepare for the journey.

She and Jan would marry at a required civil ceremony and then at a private religious ceremony held at the Wojek's. They would then travel as husband and wife to reside in Poznan with Jan's Uncle Alexandre and Aunt Patrika. Being in relatively secure Prussian German-held Poznan would place Jan out of the grasping hands of the Cossacks, and give them some time to earn money for traveling expenses. They would travel to Poznan with Kasper when he went to a horse show in March, their belongings on the wagon with his horse feed.

Suzanna nodded at the information, grateful that Jan would be safe from a cruel future that could keep him from her permanently. She did love him and want to be his wife.

"We just need to set the date for the wedding," Jan said enthusiastically. "And I've asked Josef to accompany us as well, so we will have family you know there in addition to Uncle Martin and his family. We can live near my cousins and help each other on our homesteads."

Suzanna relaxed a little at that revelation. She didn't remember Julius nor Frank that well but she did admire Josef, with his good looks and quiet ways. If Jan hadn't begun courting her, she might have pursued her attraction to Josef. It would be wonderful to have him along with them.

"Father Ignacio contacted a sympathetic judge," Jan continued, "who arranged military fulfillment documents for me and Josef, and letters of recommendation to be used as passports, so we can emigrate.

"Josef will continue to work at the coal mines until just before we depart and will meet us in Poznan to take the train to Bremerhaven, the closest German seaport. He'll travel as an assistant to Father Ignacio who will be officiating at his normal church services in Poznan."

Although she knew it wasn't her place to question her fiancé's judgment, Suzanna couldn't resist asking, "But how will we be able to afford all of this? Isn't it expensive to travel to America? How will we get there?"

Jan smiled in response, proud of his planning. "We, my future wife, will purchase our ship tickets in Poznan where the shipping company agent is located. Uncle Martin has agreed to send us the money and we will reimburse him when we can."

Suzanna inwardly frowned at that remark. Everyone knew he who lends to a friend makes an enemy, but this was family. Maybe it would work out with God's help.

"We only need to bring our baptismal and marital records, and go with the ship agent to register our emigration status at the police department. The agent will meet us at the train station to ensure we meet our train and that our luggage is properly tagged for transport to the steamship."

Suzanna blanched white again. *Train! Steamship! Blessed Mary help her.* She had never traveled by anything other than horse, farm wagon or her own bare feet.

"From Bremen," Jan continued, beaming excitedly, "it will take us about two weeks to sail across the Atlantic Ocean to Manhattan where Uncle Martin will meet us to take us to their home in Minnesota. From there we will travel to Dakota Territory to claim and establish our property before all of the free land is taken."

Although Suzanna's head was whirling with all that would need to be accomplished, she secretly hoped that maybe their move to America, as overwhelming as that was, would somehow avert her feared destiny. She had been the unlucky girl who had picked the pot containing a clump of clod last St. Andrew's Eve and she couldn't shake the foreboding she had felt since then, that she would meet an early demise as the saying foretold. She *would* be the first to marry since she caught Elizbieta's wedding veil. Despite the prayers she fervently prayed beseeching protection, the precautions she took against the evil eye, and the lilacs she placed under her pillow for sweet dreams, that night she had nightmares of a black-haired heathen crouching over her body.

Loss of Faith

Zofia slammed the door, rattling the doorframe to her cottage after she heard the news of the eminent wedding and the rumors of Jan and Suzanna's emigration to America. She didn't mind the marriage. What she did mind was the loss of business. To please her grandmother, Suzanna had chosen to wear her grandmother's wedding dress and not have a new one sewn. Foolish girl! How was a woman to make a living if people didn't use her services? Soon she would be feeling the pangs of hunger and poverty herself—or the humiliation of sitting before the church in supplication. She certainly wasn't getting any younger, and it wouldn't be long before no man would look at her with anything other than contempt or pity.

Pulling off her gloves and tailored wool coat, flinging them aside in her anger, Zofia hurried to place wood on the banked embers to get a fire going in her hearth. While making her rounds of the public houses and stores to glean news of any business opportunities, the cold January weather had penetrated her warm clothes and chilled even her blood, it seemed.

Worse, Zofia continued to fume as the kindling finally lit, Suzanna had even chosen to make it a small wedding, *curse her soul*. Most weddings had as many as ten witnesses but Suzanna was only having her younger sister Flora and Jan's cousin Josef stand up for them. And Flora would not need a new dress either. The attendants and families would be wearing each family's traditional festival costumes!

Jan and Suzanna were going to be rich! Why not squander money now? Zofia questioned. Whatever happened to the common tradition of "*Zastaw się, a postaw się,*": "Show off, even with borrowed money," even if you starved for six months? *What was happening with this younger generation?* Such inconsiderate actions would only bring Polish businesses to their knees. Money, or going into debt, was never a consideration on such an important occasion.

Zofia filled a kettle with water to heat for tea, as her temper continued to simmer. This was the second time she had lost commerce from those two families. If the neighbors followed their example, she would soon be starving herself! And that would never do. *Well, they would learn*, she thought, as the tea kettle began to whistle.

As she drank her soothing tea, she quietly made plans to meet with a Russian friend of hers. Business was business, no matter where it came from. They would regret being so selfish.

❦

Jan flung the gathered bundles of ash saplings beside the bristles from birch twigs and the thin pieces of willow wood on the barn floor. That should be enough supplies for broom makings. After they bound them together, he and Suzanna would peddle them for 3 grosz each.

Jan shook his head. Work had been hard to find. He had hired out his labor for odd jobs when he could find them and he had even worked a few days in the coal mine with Josef, when a mate came up sick. He'd also moved his trap-lines to a new location and hoped the animal tracks he had seen would bring in more bounty. Money would be tight but with God's help they would make it.

Josef, meanwhile, laid down his straight flush with a grin on his face. He'd done it. He had won the cowhides. Now he could make horsewhips from the stripped leather. They would bring a good price at the market.

"You horse's ass!" Kasper exclaimed as he threw down his losing hand. "You are much too lucky tonight, Josef. That's enough for me. You'll have my best stallion next if I don't stop now!"

"You can afford it," Josef teased his old friend, downing the rest of his vodka. "It looks like the horse flesh business is good." Josef had known Kasper since his work in the stables. Kasper would save his best horses for the lord's perusal, and was richly rewarded for his efforts. He had also taught Josef many tips for dealing with horses; one of the most important was to never whip a horse for becoming frightened at any object by the roadside. He taught him that if the horse saw a stump, a log, or a heap of anything in the road, he should allow the horse time to examine it and smell it to learn to lose its fear of unknown objects. Kasper knew everything there was to know about horses and freely taught Josef all he could in their long relationship.

"War is good for my business," Kasper nodded, "but you'll want to tread carefully. The Russian slime are still on the prowl for fresh blood."

"No problem there," Josef replied. "I'll be off the streets working double shifts for the next couple of months to make enough to get to America."

"America. They say the streets are paved with gold. I wish I was still young enough to risk it. But I am too set in my ways. You, however, with your luck and strong back, will be wealthy in no time!"

Josef laughed as he rolled up the cowhides to better handle them on his walk back to the coal mine barracks. With a slap on his back, Kasper watched with a concerned expression as Josef set off. Those kids had more problems than they knew about but there was no sense worrying them over the details. Since they were good young men who deserved a chance at a better life, he would handle it.

❦

"These men never think beyond their money pouches!" Helen declared as she expertly wove the wet oak sapwood over and under the ribs of the last trunk she and Suzanna were preparing from scavenged and treated oak branches. Suzanna had just finished attaching the handles to the sides of the other trunk to make it easier to carry. The marriage chest built by her grandfather, painted with the traditional fertility and wedding flowers by her grandmother, would hold Suzanna's dowry linens and their work clothes. The two oak baskets would contain their cooking and eating utensils and Jan's and Josef's essential tools, in addition to a few precious seeds and bulbs to make their house a home.

Suzanna inwardly lamented that they were taking only the barest necessities with them in order to have money for traveling expenses and supplies once they reached their new home. If they had stayed in Poland, a whole treasure-trove of wedding gifts would have been given to them. As it was, they were requesting money in lieu of presents. It was simply too expensive to ship goods to America, and they desperately needed funds more than they did material goods until they were settled.

"You must understand that men are completely different from women, Suzanna," her mother said, aware of her daughter's silent grieving for the completely different life that she would experience compared to most Polish women. "All they think of is money and how to make a living. Free land is a miracle for them but men often overlook the needs of their women in their desire to achieve their goals. You must forgive Jan for his shortsightedness," she said in commiseration. "He means well but it has ever been thus.

"I know you are disappointed to be moving so far from your family," she continued, "but a wise woman must often sacrifice her desires for the good of the family, just as Manya and Josef's mothers are doing by giving their blessing to their sons' desire to leave Poland. With war in the making, it is the best choice, although it is certainly not what they would have wished for their sons. Both men promise to send money back to their families—as is just. They will not shirk their responsibility to the families that reared them, even if they are going to another country. The well-being of the entire family must always be considered. Remember God's words in 1 Timothy 5:8, "But if anyone does not provide for his relatives, and especially for members of his household, he has denied the faith and is worse than an unbeliever."

Suzanna nodded mechanically as her mother continued. "But as with bearing children," Helen glanced quickly at Suzanna, who as a farm girl, knew the facts of life, but still blushed at the comment in her innocence, "a little discomfort can be endured if the long-term goals are worth it. In this case the risk of failure is worth the hardships experienced to achieve success. You must look on moving to America as a blessing, Suzanna. Although we will miss you, we will stay in contact through letters. And God willing, we will one day see our grandchildren," Helen assured her.

"Yes, mother," Suzanna automatically agreed. "I sincerely hope God will bless us and make it so." Suzanna didn't want to think about the distance she would be from her family. It only made her heartsick and nervous. Soon she would be sharing her wedding bed with Jan and that made her anxious enough. She had heard only men enjoyed marital intimacy and it was a duty women had to endure. She hoped it wouldn't be too painful. She inwardly shuddered and decided that she should take her mother's advice and concentrate on the new family she and Jan would be creating. She did so want children. Anything was worth that result.

United Dreams

Saturday, February 5, 1870 was finally here. *Her wedding day*, Suzanna smiled happily. She had been waiting for this day her entire life and she was going to enjoy it, even if it did signify the end of her freedom. The maiden's evening had been full of merriment with all of her female friends and relatives unbraiding her hair, giving her advice about how to have a good marriage and teasing her about what to expect in the wedding bed. They had baked the wedding cake and decorated her parent's barn for the Roman Catholic ceremony, dinner, and dance.

Each woman had given her at least one of their favorite recipes and embroidered linens that she had added to her marriage chest. She and Jan would spend their wedding night at the groom's house per tradition and would return the following day to Suzanna's parent's house for the *poprawiny* before they proceeded to Poznan. Although traditional Polish weddings frequently lasted for several festivity-filled days, they had shortened theirs to just two to avoid Cossack notice.

Jan looked handsome in his traditional black felt flower-trimmed hat, black overshirt and gold pantaloons with matching wide belt when he arrived in the flower-bedecked horse carriage. He smiled broadly as Suzanna emerged from her home. She was a vision in a white linen lace-trimmed veil crowned with attached flowers. Her wide-sleeved lace-trimmed blouse was complimented by a variegated green skirt hemmed in black cloth with *wesele* cutout floral patterns. Her beauty made Jan's body pound with desire. When he and Suzanna knelt in front of her parents, they were greeted with bread, salt, and wine so they would never know hunger and would prosper. Her parents gave them their blessing and Jan received a gold chain since "every young bull should be kept on a chain" and Suzanna received a gold-edged print of the Madonna and child to remind her of her role as nurturer of their new family.

The courthouse civil ceremony went quickly and the band-led convoy of vehicles was halted by nearby neighbors wielding various implements blockading the return route to the Wojek's. Only when Jan bartered vodka with them was he allowed to pass the *bramas,* gates, and proceed to take his bride to the unsanctioned Catholic wedding ceremony.

The barn rafters were hidden by brightly colored paper flowers with a small altar set at the far end of the room. Flora and Josef stood before the altar as Jan was escorted by his mother and Suzanna by her father through the throng of friends and relatives.

"We are gathered together on this happy occasion to join this man and woman in eternal matrimony in the sight of God," Father Ignacio intoned as the ceremony began. "Let us remember the words of Saint Peter when he advised brides as follows: 'Likewise, wives, be subject to your own husbands, so that even if some do not obey the word, they may be won without a word by the conduct of their wives, when they see your respectful and pure conduct. Do not let your adorning be external—the braiding of hair and the putting on of gold jewelry, or the clothing you wear—but let your adorning be the hidden person of the heart with the imperishable beauty of a gentle and quiet spirit, which in God's sight is very precious.' For this is how the holy women who hoped in God used to adorn themselves, by submitting to their own husbands.

"In Proverbs we find that an excellent wife is described as more precious than jewels. 'The heart of her husband trusts in her, and he will have no lack of gain. She does him good, and not harm, all the days of her life. She seeks wool and flax, and works with willing hands.' With a certainty we know that man was not created for woman, but woman for man. But husbands must love their wives, as Christ loved the church and gave himself up for her.

"Let us now join this man and this woman. Repeat after me: 'I, Jan, take you, Suzanna, as my wedded wife and I promise you love, honor, and respect: to be faithful to you and not to forsake you until death do us part, so help me God, one in the Holy Trinity and all the Saints.' " "Suzanna, take this ring as a sign of my love and fidelity. In the name of the Father, and of the Son, and of

The Eagle's Nest

the Holy Spirit." Jan repeated the vows and placed the simple band on Suzanna's right hand. Suzanna followed suit, promising to be a devoted wife and helpmate to her husband.

"And God blessed them," Father Ignacio continued, "And God said to them, 'Be fruitful and multiply and fill the earth and subdue it and have dominion over the fish of the sea and over the birds of the heavens and over every living thing that moves on the earth.' *"Mozesz pocalowac panne mloda"* (You may now kiss the bride). A cheer went up from the crowd as Jan passionately claimed his wife's lips. Suzanna's body pleasantly throbbed with unfamiliar sensations as she accepted her husband's possessive kiss.

When he finally stopped to catch his breath, they walked to the rear of the room as the guests tossed one-*grosz* coins at them. Jan and Suzanna merrily picked up the coins and placed them in a small bag to be kept for the rest of their lives as a good luck token. Their wedding reception, their "happy occasion," had officially begun.

After greeting their guests and accepting their well wishes, the bride and bridegroom sat at the dinner table surrounded by their guests, the most important being seated next to them. The guests held up their glasses filled with vodka and chanted "Bitter, bitter, bitter" indicating that the taste is not good enough until the groom once again kisses the bride. The crowd erupted in cheers and laughter as Jan eagerly complied with tradition.

Eating and drinking proceeded merrily with an occasional drunk choir accompanying the band throughout the evening. The band harmonized with well-loved songs such as "A Girl Went to a Forest" and "Mountaineer, Aren't You Feeling Sad?" Many guests paid the band to hear their favorite songs, and pinned money to the bride's gown when they danced with her. One traditional song reiterated their hopes for the new couple:

"May the star of prosperity never stop shining for them

Never stop shining, never stop shining

And in this new shared life

May it shine even brighter!"

As the crowd danced with linked-arms around the bride and groom the band played:

"A hundred years, a hundred years may they live and live and live.
Once again, once again may they live and live and live,
One hundred years."

Many guests were entirely drunk by the end of the evening after *gorzko* was shouted for the newlyweds to kiss repeatedly after the band played,

"Bitter vodka, bitter vodka
Need to make it sweeter
The Groom will kiss the Bride
It won't do them any harm."

Jan and Suzanna secretly drank water after the first few toasts, so they wouldn't become as inebriated as most of their guests. At midnight the *oczepiny* began with a drum roll by the band. Suzanna was placed on a chair in the middle of the dance floor facing the guests. Flora, Manya, Suzanna's godmother and grandmothers surrounded Suzanna with lit candles as Helen removed the bridal veil. As the band played the song "*Serdeczna Matko*," Beloved Mother, Helen placed a *czepek*, cap, on the brides head, and Suzanna was now officially considered a married woman.

She smiled with pride as her younger floral-crowned sisters presented her with a ribbon-bedecked broom and a brightly decorated apron. She immediately put on the apron, then tossed her wedding veil to the single women in the crowd. Flora caught Suzanna's veil then Josef grappled with another bachelor for Jan's tossed tie.

At the prompting of the music, Jan and Suzanna then began the traditional wedding *oberek*, an energetic, spinning, twirling dance around the dance floor. The thoroughly energized guests joined them then exuberantly followed them to Jan's home, serenading the newlyweds as they traveled along.

When finally alone after much teasing and drunken advice, Jan kissed and slowly soothed away Suzanna's fears and consummated their new life together in the early hours of the morning. Each was completely satisfied by their chosen mate and deeply pleased to be in the arms of the other.

Escape

Their journey to Poznan had been blessedly uneventful due to Kasper's good business sense and open ears. Once he had learned from an inebriated Zofia that the young couple wouldn't make it past the border, hinting of her "good" friendship with a certain Russian border guard, he had chosen another less frequently used route to avoid detection. With winter still in full force, Kasper had hidden their trunks under the forage hay for his horses while Jan and Suzanna pretended to be his employees, traveling along to help Kasper sell the brooms and horsewhips in the Poznan marketplace.

"I am so frightened," Suzanna whispered to Jan where they were nestled together in the back of the wagon as they approached the border checkpoint. "What if we are caught? What will happen if they question our papers?"

"Trust in God, Suzanna. Nothing will happen. Kasper is well-known at the border crossings. If he says all will be well, all will be well. Just pretend that you are asleep," he responded quietly, trying not to show his own nervousness. They could be imprisoned for leaving the country without Russian-approved travel papers.

Kasper slowed the wagon with his horses tied to the wagon, trailing behind them, "Whoa," he said as he reached the guardhouse.

"Traveling a little late tonight, aren't you, Kasper?" the guard called out as he recognized Kasper.

"Yes, no thanks to my new help," he replied as he nodded to Suzanna and Jan in the wagon. "They can't tell time or read a clock properly," he said with a grimace.

The guard laughed, looking over the two hands, "It's hard to find good help these days. These young kids are so lazy. They don't know what a hard day's labor is!"

Kasper nodded, agreeably, "Isn't that the truth? It will probably take me a while to hammer the routine into their thick heads, but they'll do once I get them properly trained with a lick or two."

The guard nodded, agreeing, "That's the only way they seem to learn."

Jumping down from the wagon seat, Kasper pulled out a bottle of vodka, and waved it at the guard. "It's damn cold out here. Can I offer you a nip?"

The guard looked greedily at the bottle. It *was* cold out and he wanted to return to his warm fire. He reached out his hand, and took the bottle from Kasper, immediately opening it and taking a deep swallow. As he began to hand it back to Kasper, he waved it back to him, "No," Kasper said. "You keep it. These two have made me late enough. I'd best be on my way or we won't make it to the sale. I'll probably have to wake up the stable hands, as it is."

The guard nodded, as the wind grew brisk again, he waved them forward. "Okay, off with you. It's too cold to linger out here. See you next time."

Their traveling credentials had been completely unquestioned when Kasper offered to warm up the cold, immediately congenial guard. They all breathed a sigh of relief, not realizing that they each had been holding their breaths in anxiety.

"Praise God," Jan muttered, as Kasper whipped the horses into action, and he squeezed Suzanna's shoulders. "We are on our way to America."

❖

Once in German territory, they boarded Kasper's horses at a local stable for the night and quickly reached Uncle Alexandre's and Aunt Patrika's home. Chilled to the bone from the frosty wind that had accompanied them throughout their journey, Patrika invited them in with relief and open arms, offering them a place by the fire. After serving them a hardy lentil soup accompanied by plenty of dark bread, Kasper accepted Alexandre's and Patrika's offer of lodging for the night.

Happy to have been an angel in disguise for the young couple's bid for freedom, the next morning he told them of their near betrayal by the vindictive Zofia. "She's turned into a hard woman since the war. Losing her husband stole the goodness out of her," he explained as he shook his head in sadness.

Jan and Suzanna were shocked by Zofia's attempted betrayal. Some people were becoming mean and dishonorable in their fear and poverty. "Do you think she has endangered Josef's trip?" Jan asked in concern.

"No, Josef and Father Ignacio shouldn't have any problems crossing either. I greased a few Russian fingers of my own for their safe journey."

"I don't know how we will ever be able to repay you, my friend," Jan said to Kasper.

"Cherish the freedom you have been given and help others when you have the opportunity. Remember the families you leave behind," he responded sincerely, "as times may be rough for them." With a final wave goodbye, he left to gather his horses.

❈

Poznan had spread beyond its initial fortified, wall-enclosed city and castle, which had once been the capital of Greater Poland, the home of the King of Poland, and the seat of local dukes. The city had flourished as educational and political institutions were founded, and more crafts and tradesmen built along the Warta River.

Wars, plagues, and political agendas decimated its population over time until Prussian rule over Poznan was established during the second partition of Poland. It then once again became home to significant trade, transportation, and German military forces centered on the Fort Winiary citadel and its associated 18 forts.

Josef and Father Ignacio did arrive safely several days later and the Riskes were overjoyed to see them at Sunday service at Poznan Cathedral, the oldest cathedral in Poland. After their leave-taking of Father Ignacio, wherever they went, Jan, Suzanna, and Josef could not avoid the bustling presence of German military personnel. Avoiding any contact as much as possible, they peddled their brooms and horsewhips in the Poznan marketplace. Exhaling a huge sigh of relief at their profits, their next stop was with the Norddeutscher Lloyd's ship agent where their papers were inspected, and their train and ship tickets purchased. The following day they celebrated their success and participated in an ancient Polish festival.

The return of the storks from the warmer climates heralded the return of spring and a subsequent custom, *topienie Marzanny,* the drowning of *Marzanna*, ensued with great enthusiasm on March 21st, the first day of spring. *Marzanna,* a straw figure representing death, winter, disease, and all evil, was dressed in women's clothing and carried in procession around the village, from door to door, to chase away evil spirits. Once each house was cleansed, *Marzanna* was carried to the river bank, burned, and while still in flames, thrown into the Warta River. Everyone then ran home as fast as possible, but as carefully as they could, because it was believed that anyone who fell while running home would die that same year.

Jan and Josef laughingly held Suzanna upright between them as they sped back to Uncle Alexandre's house to enjoy a festive meal that Aunt Patrika had prepared. With equal anticipation and sadness they toasted their eminent journey and filled their bellies with duck blood soup, savoring the precious raisins included as a sweet complement to the nutritious entree.

The Journey

Jan, Suzanna, and Josef watched as their three sturdy trunks survived the assault of the cargo-men as they flung them onto a heavily laden net in preparation to be hoisted onto the steamship *Main*. It was a cold, blustery Saturday, March 26, 1870. The wind off the water had women drawing their shawls more tightly to their bodies, and men shoving their hands into their armpits. With luck, they would reach Southampton, England within two days to take on more passengers, then depart for America on the 29th.

Suzanna's stomach flipped as she gazed at the ship that would be their home for at least two weeks. *God give me strength,* she thought as she wrenched her eyes from that imposing sight to watch the throng of people around her—although that was no more reassuring.

The steamship *Main* had accommodations for 70 passengers in 1st class, 100 in 2nd class, and 600 in steerage with a crew of 105, and all were busily preparing for departure. Sailors scurried about their duties, and anxious mothers tried to keep their children in tow while the men confirmed final arrangements and received repeated assurances from ship agents. Well-wishers and those to be left behind were all speaking metaphorically "in tongues"—German, Polish and other languages she didn't recognize. And the costumes they wore! There were men in tights with short skirts, others in homespun close-fit britches or baggy pants. Heads were adorned with turbans, feathers, veils, and hats of every shape and material. Women wore shawls, scarves, and brightly colored embroidered vests. Each carried parcels filled with the necessities they would need for the journey. Since Suzanna grew up very sheltered in her small village, she had never seen such a variety of humankind in one place.

Satisfied that their luggage with all of their worldly possessions was disappearing into the bowels of the *Main*, Jan hooked his thumbs beneath his suspenders and interrupted Suzanna's reverie. "You know, you look as lovely as the day we married, Mrs. Riske."

Suzanna blushed, embarrassed but grateful that Jan took her mind off her fears and her unsettled stomach. She immediately gently admonished him, "*Oj*, what will Josef think, Jan?"

Josef silently agreed with his cousin but grinned at Suzanna, "Don't worry, Suzanna. I'll pretend I didn't hear my lovesick cousin's comments."

Suzanna was dressed in a dark blue gown with a removable crochet collar. The fit of the gown accentuated her slender waist and her 163-cm petite frame. Her golden braids encircled her head and the hand-stitched dress perfectly accentuated her matching eye color. She used her shawl to cover her head and shoulders from the brisk wind.

Jan looked at his towering 188-cm, broad-shouldered, slim-hipped cousin and responded, "Once we get settled in America, we'll find you a fine filly of your own. Of course, we'll have to get you to talk to a woman first," Jan teased the perennially shy Josef.

Jan and Suzanna were comfortable in their new marriage, although all of the changes, preparations, and uncertainty had been stressful. They buoyed each other up when one would falter and question their decisions. Ultimately they felt their plan was the only one possible for their future wellbeing. Martin had kept good on his promise and had sent them each the $15 needed for their ship tickets. They had mailed him their arrival information so he could meet them in New York as their sponsor.

"Just think, within six weeks, we may be breaking our own land! God has surely blessed us," Jan smiled broadly, although he was secretly anxious to enter the ship. Luck had been with them so far, but he would only feel completely safe once they were on their way.

With all of the preparations for the wedding and the voyage, time had flown quickly and their final parting had been painful. Suzanna would miss her family dreadfully. Her knees shook at the mere thought of climbing aboard that vast vessel that would take her away from everything she had ever known. But

Suzanna was determined to persevere. She would not shame her husband by showing her misgivings. Just as the strength of the heartwood for the rims of the trunks had been tightly woven to sustain calamity, Suzanna had to believe the strength of their families' love would continue to bind them together no matter the distance between them.

"Look, they are lining up to board the ship. Let's get in line so we can get good berths. I'll get mine," Josef said to Jan, "while you and Suzanna get settled." Single men would be housed separately, at the opposite end of the ship from the single women. Married couples and families with children were to reside in the center of the ship's third-class accommodations. All silently prayed that the frightening living conditions in steerage, of which they had been warned, were exaggerations. *This is a fairly new vessel, only two years old, with improved accommodations*, Suzanna mentally assured herself. *Surely horrors will not sail with us*, she thought as she braced herself for the hardest walk of her life.

Suzanna let out a deep sigh, trying to release the tension she was feeling as they entered the bowels of the ship. She just hoped that God would take better care of them on their voyage than He had of Poland. Oh how she wished she could be as certain as Jan that God was in control. She often felt that the Devil had somehow usurped God's power in Poland. Maybe it *was* better to go somewhere the Devil wasn't.

❦

Steerage was a crowded mass of bodies, each eagerly claiming a likely bunk. Two-high, 6 by 6 foot berths with thin mattresses lined each side of the ship with sections in the middle for families with children. Interspersed throughout the sections were barrels of water, stockpiles of wood, and stoves set in bins of sand. Although there were privies on the steerage deck, night pots were stored beneath all of the bunks and the aisles were strewn with sawdust.

Stewards and mates directed passengers to berths, advising them to tie down extra baggage under or beside bunks. Suzanna and Jan were allotted an upper berth, where they stored the basket of cheese, summer sausage, bread, and apples that Aunt Patrika had given them. They were glad to be out of the way and to have an elevated view of their surroundings. Coming from poverty, most steerage passengers were accustomed to sharing space with others, and were used to worse sleeping conditions, so they quickly settled into their crowded quarters.

After being assigned his berth with a friendly bunkmate from Berlin, Josef hurried to the deck to have one last look at the land he would be leaving behind. Eager to be on his way, Josef anxiously paced the steerage deck as they set sail. The mild sway of the deck caused by the 12-knot cruising speed had him trying to convince his legs he hadn't imbibed any alcohol.

The view was a satisfying one as he watched the spider's web of ship masts and land gradually diminish in size behind them. He was thrilled to be out of the coal-mine's grime and fetid air, and equally relieved to be free from the Cossacks. Although nervous about being on a basically hollow cork on the ocean, he had to admit the sea air was invigorating, and to him, smelled of hope.

All of the hard work of the last several months has been worth it, he thought as he watched the wake of the ship stream behind them. The remainder of his meager wages was evenly distributed in each of his boots for safe-keeping. They had estimated it would cost them about $14 each traveling and living expenses to reach the American interior. Although they didn't have that much, they hoped Martin could help them if they needed it. If nothing else, they could always hire out their labor to earn any needed money.

A shrill whistle brought the *Main* passengers to a brief orientation by the 1st mate, after which they toured the ship on their own and enjoyed the short trip to Southampton. Sailing was smooth, and after docking briefly to take on mail packets and more passengers, their days soon settled into a pattern.

The German company ran a disciplined ship and expected passengers to abide by iron-clad safety restrictions. Passengers were required to stay below deck after dark and during inclement weather. There was to be no tobacco or pipe smoking in steerage, nor were candles allowed anywhere on the ship. Hanging paraffin lamps provided lighting and were lit below deck after dark.

Fires were lit in the stoves each day at 6 a.m., and every passenger not hindered by sickness or physical impediment was expected to arise no later than 7 a.m. Night pots were emptied overboard and cleaned first thing every morning, and passengers swept the deck and under bunks in their quarters before breakfast, tossing the sweepings overboard and applying fresh sawdust.

Each morning men rotated the duty of replacing the necessary fuel in the lamps and water in the barrels that were tied down in the center aisle of each section. A group of passengers also assisted the 1st cook in distributing the meals. A breakfast of tea, coffee or chocolate, bread or biscuits, and butter was served promptly at 9 a.m. At 1 p.m., a dinner of soup, and beef or pork with potatoes, was provided (with the addition of plum pudding on Sundays), and supper began at 6 p.m. sharp with a repeat of the breakfast menu. All eating utensils were washed after use using the barrels provided.

The stoves were extinguished at 8 p.m. and passengers were abed by 10 p.m. when the lamps were extinguished. Many passengers made their berths comfortable with their own bedding and entertained their children or exchanged news and plans with their shipmates. Everyone was excited to be on their way to the prospects of America and the din of 600 people was a backdrop that would be their constant companion throughout the journey.

New Beginnings

The ocean demonstrated its sovereignty the 7th day into the journey. A raging storm arose that birthed 30 foot waves and made the passenger decks treacherous, confining the passengers to their quarters. During the worst of the pitching, Suzanna and Jan had clung to their upper berth, arising only when necessary. Huddled together, they had eaten the biscuit and water rations, and slept in their clothes, reassuring each other that their guardian angels were watching over them. They were delighted when one of the passengers brought out his fiddle and allayed their fears with his melodies.

On Sunday, when all were required to be on deck in clean clothes to observe the Sabbath, the swells and rain caused services to be cancelled but the 1st mate entered each section and read from the Bible. All silently prayed that the repeated scripture, "*Do not fear, for I am with you*" (Isaiah 41:10), was true.

Suzanna's nausea had not dissipated since she had been on the *Main* and as the stench from night-pots and the effluence of those with weak stomachs steadily rose during their two-day confinement, Suzanna's discomfort increased. She hoped that she wasn't taking ill and that it was only seasickness she was enduring. Jan was concerned and solicitous, but there was little he could do but feed her bits of food and distract her from her distress.

The berths around them held primarily young couples. Greta and her husband Carl were from a small village outside of Leipzig, Prussia-Germany. They were traveling to Kansas to homestead with Carl's older brother. Greta was 7 months pregnant, and she and Suzanna had become acquainted in the long lines to retrieve their meals.

As Suzanna bent over a slop bucket yet another time, Greta commiserated with her, "I was so ill the first few months of my pregnancy, I thought I would never eat again, but thank God, the nausea finally stopped. Anyone would be ill in here now though."

Stunned, Suzanna wiped her face with a damp handkerchief then scooped some sawdust from the floor into the bucket to help dispel the vile stench. *Could it be?* When the ship finally emerged from the stormy weather, but her nausea continued, Jan insisted Suzanna see the doctor on board. After a few questions and a brief examination, the doctor confirmed her suspicions. She was pregnant.

Jan's worried expression changed to delight when she gave him the good news. In his relief and exuberance, he swung her around in a circle then hugged her tightly to his chest, "I am to be a father? Praise God." He held her at arm's length, "Are you sure you are all right? Is there anything we need to do?"

Suzanna shook her head, pleased at his reaction, "The doctor said the nausea is completely normal and should go away soon. He said eating small amounts of bread and drinking a little tea should settle my stomach, but that there is nothing to worry about. He said I am perfectly healthy but I should rest when I feel tired and get as much fresh air as possible."

After her revelation to Jan, Suzanna's own mind remained unsettled. She tried to wrap her mind around the fact that she was pregnant. Although thrilled to know she would be a mother, her hand went involuntarily to her stomach and she mentally checked the state of her body. She felt no momentous changes in her body. *You would think something would feel different*, she thought, but it didn't. *Would being pregnant be painful?* she wondered. She tried to remember all of the times her mother was with child. She knew the birth itself would be uncomfortable, but her mother had behaved completely normally during her pregnancies and had never complained. After each birth, her mother was always up the next day, routinely suckling the newborn as she went about tending to the rest of her family. Suzanna decided she would have to talk to Greta.

The next morning as she and Greta were on deck airing out their bedding while others hung clean clothes to dry, Suzanna broached the subject. Greta was excited at her news and reassured Suzanna that as the baby grew, it would kick and move occasionally but that there was no pain involved. She said that she would get an occasional backache if she overworked, but it was nothing that couldn't be handled.

Reassured, Suzanna relaxed and noticed that her nausea did dissipate significantly when they were on deck after she learned to focus on the horizon, not the sea, to keep her equilibrium. The endless ocean seemed to stretch forever around them and the occasional glimpse of icebergs captivated her attention. For the remainder of the trip, after their chores were finished, they bundled up against the chilly weather and took daily strolls with Josef to partake of the fresh sea air. Josef's bunkmate, Victor, frequently joined them.

"What brings you to America, Victor?" Jan asked him, as he noticed a group of men surreptitiously throwing dice near the life boats. Jan quickly guided Suzanna away from the group. Not that he had anything against gambling, but card playing or any form of gambling was forbidden on the ship since it could easily lead to arguments. It was better to avoid any possible strife.

"My older sister lost her husband, God rest his soul, in the American War Between the States. He was a member of the Pennsylvania Brigade. Toward the end of the war they were drafting men up to 50-years-old, which is how he entered. Luckily the Union held and the country is stable again but in all of the turmoil, it took some time to learn news of his demise. I'm traveling to Philadelphia where she lives with her six children to help run their property," Victor quietly responded. "It's been ten years since I've seen her, but a woman needs her family beside her."

Jan nodded his agreement. "I'm sorry to hear of your loss, Victor. It is good of you to help her. We lost a cousin at Gettysburg as well. He was determined to defend what he believed to be right and gave his life doing so."

Victor was surprised by Jan's remarks. It was unusual for an immigrant to be willing to fight for his new country, though many did.

"America has been going through chaos as much as Europe has it seems and unfortunately Germany and Russia are starting up again—and I want no part of it," Jan continued. "I am no coward and fighting for your own country I fully support. But when your country no longer exists, then fighting is throwing your life away. Everyone has a role in life. Mine, I believe, is to feed people so they can lead good lives."

"Well, Josef tells me it sounds like you'll have that opportunity in Dakota Territory," Victor asserted. "America is still a large untamed country with abundant opportunity for those willing to put forth the effort to succeed. The slavery issue was unfortunate but it looks like they have that handled. I personally think buying and selling human beings is a despicable business that is unworthy of any country. Thankfully President Lincoln, God rest his soul, freed those unfortunate people. But America still has challenges. What to do with the native Indians is one of them."

"What have you heard?" Jan asked eagerly.

Victor tempered his response as he noticed Suzanna's eyes widened in concern, "Their essentially nomadic lifestyle made it difficult for them to live near Europeans who settle in one place. Most of them are on reservations now but there are some who are still free. There are forts in all of the settled territories, however, and the cavalry has been able to handle any issues that have arisen."

They nodded as they passed a woman practicing English words with her young son. "Thank you," she said in English, "which means what in German?" she asked her son in German.

"*Danka*," he said immediately.

"Very good! You'll soon be speaking English like an expert," she said as she smiled at him. Jan and Suzanna both beamed at the rosy-cheeked youngster. Soon they would have a youngster, too.

"They sound like us, Victor! We can't thank you enough for helping us learn a little English, too. We all face challenges," Jan commented, patting Suzanne's hand, "but with a little faith and friends like you, we should succeed." Victor agreed. He had taken to these friendly Poles and their determination to find a better life for themselves. He would stay in contact with them when possible once they reached the new country.

Through the Gauntlet

The *Main* reached port Friday, April 8, with 642 immigrants aboard. Its arrival at Castlerock, located at the tip of Manhattan, was preceded by being pulled by tugboats into the lower bay of New York harbor. The pilot boarded her off Sandy Hook and guided her to drop anchor in front of the official residence of the Quarantine Officer. The Health Officer's barge, embellished with a yellow flag, proceeded to the *Main* bringing the health inspection crew who immediately boarded the ship.

All of the immigrants were mustered upon the main deck to pass before the Health Officer. He determined quickly if any sick were among the well passengers. If any were ill, they were directed to the side to be examined to learn the nature of their disease.

Jan, Josef, and Suzanna watched nervously as those before them filed by the doctor. He marked questionable person's clothing with chalk figures that were evidence of what needed to be further inspected. On some he marked an "L," "E," or "X."

"Victor, do you know what those mean?" asked Josef.

"The steward told me that "L" stands for lame, "E" means eye problems, an "H" is for heart disease, and the scariest is an "X" for mental problems. We're all healthy. We only need to worry if anyone has a contagious disease such as typhoid or yellow fever. If that happens, then the whole ship has to go into quarantine and be fumigated, and everyone is transferred on to a hospital ship to be examined. Pray the ship gets a clean bill of health and we can proceed to the dock," Victor replied.

"I've been told that on the hospital ship if they find lice, their heads are shaved. If they have skin problems, they must bathe in disinfectants. Eye problems, which may indicate trachoma, and is contagious, can lead to blindness. The steward said they look under the eyelids using a buttonhook for that particular disease."

Suzanna gasped in horror, "God help those poor people."

"Don't worry, Mrs. Riske," Victor responded, "America is very advanced medically and most of the patients can be treated. Again, let us hope that our medical papers are stamped 'passed.'"

The review took most of the morning but the ship was judged "not contagious" so the passengers' baggage then underwent a thorough examination. The Custom-house Inspector and his crew were familiar with the behavior of smugglers who pretended to be immigrants to conceal goods and avoid paying duty taxes. As fast each as item was examined it was sent over the side onto a barge followed by its owner. When the customs agents finished inspecting the luggage the barge proceeded to Castle Garden.

The journey to the dock was swift and all immigrants were grateful to have passed finally onto American soil. Some immediately knelt down and thanked God for their safe delivery from the sea and the dire circumstances that had caused them to emigrate. They were quickly marshaled into either the customs area for further inspections or into the rotunda of Castle Garden. When they entered the reception area, passengers were divided into sections by language where clerks with expertise in that tongue sat behind desks to continue the required immigration examinations.

Each immigrant had to perform a mental test, such as counting backward from 20 or solving simple puzzles. They then were asked legal questions such as "have you been in prison," or "do you have money or a job waiting for you." When their answers were met with approval, their names, vital information, and destinations were recorded. The murmur of responses in many languages was punctuated with exclamations of delight and relief as families reunited, or anguish, as entry was denied into the new land.

Confidant now that they were in America, Jan and Josef scanned the faces of the crowds of citizens beyond the barrier looking for their Uncle Martin. Not seeing him, Josef decided to take advantage of being able to convert their foreign coin into greenbacks near the telegraph office in the building while Jan and

Suzanna kept their place in the long lines. There he learned they could contact friends or even have a letter written and mailed for them, if need be. Elbowing his way through the noisy, bustling area, he made his way back to where the questions were being asked and fearfully answered by the immigrants.

Those passing muster were directed to the weighing room for their baggage to be weighed, which had to be no more than 80 pounds for transportation. Once their freight charges were paid and the travelers received a check for their baggage, which was then sent to a steamboat or railroad depot free of charge. The immigrants learned that their baggage could be delivered to other parts of the city for a fair rate, or it could be left in a storeroom to be retrieved later, as well. Castle Garden agents continually warned immigrants against the "sharpers" who tried to cheat or steal from the ignorant.

None of that concerned the Riskes, however, as they waited in anticipation for their benefactor, their savior, their muse: Uncle Martin. Jan, Suzanna, and Josef continued to scan the crowd eagerly for his welcome face.

Diverted

Jan, Suzanna, and Josef had passed all of their inspections by late afternoon but were still awaiting the arrival of Uncle Martin. They took advantage of the free lunch counter established for the destitute, where fresh bread and water was set out for those who were still waiting to pass the "golden gates" to the island of New York.

Earlier they had said their goodbyes to Victor and promised to stay in touch when he headed for his train. They began becoming nervous when the rotunda gradually emptied and Martin had yet to appear.

"Perhaps he didn't receive our letter with our arrival date," Suzanna suggested anxiously. "What will we do if he doesn't show up?" A sponsor had to vouch for them or they would be returned to Poland, and no letter had been waiting for them that plans had changed.

"We had better ask. It is getting late, we are all exhausted and we can't stay here," Jan responded reluctantly.

He walked to the desk of the Polish agent who had helped them earlier. The clerk was speaking in German to a well-dressed woman in her early 50s.

"How can I help you?" he asked when Jan approached.

"Our sponsor has not yet arrived. I'm not sure what we can do."

"You have several options," the agent responded. "You can go to Ward's Island until he arrives. Or you can visit the Labor Exchange to see if they have any openings for work you can perform in the city. What type of work have you done before?"

"Farming, primarily. We are headed to Dakota Territory to farm there. My wife is pregnant and we need to get settled before the baby arrives. My cousin has worked with horses and in coal mines, but we have no desire to stay in New York."

The woman who had been speaking with the agent perked up and looked the three over when she heard the word 'coal.' Both Jan and Josef were sturdy, strong young men in the prime of life. The Polish woman was pretty, although slightly pale, no doubt from her delicate condition. She was here looking for potential laborers since the Civil War had claimed so many young men.

"You've worked in coal mines overseas?" she asked in German.

"Yes, Josef and I both have," Jan responded, motioning Josef to join them.

"I could get you closer to your destination if you agree to my sponsorship. My husband owns a coal mining company in Pennsylvania, where there are 1700 square miles of coal producing counties. It is a mountainous area with elevations ranging from 600 to 1600 feet high. The mine we work is in the southern fields near Schuylkill, not far from Pottsville."

"What type of coal do you mine?" Josef asked.

"We mine anthracite coal."

Josef nodded, the more expensive stuff with a high carbon content that produces only a little black smoke and soot when burned, making it ideal for heating homes.

"There is some bituminous coal, which burns dirtier but is cheaper than anthracite, so we sell that to industries. We supply the energy for the majority of the eastern railroads, various other industries and nearly all the housing markets in the eastern United States," she boasted. "Have you worked with those coals before?"

"Yes, both," Josef replied.

"Good," she nodded, "then maybe we can come to an arrangement. You two men would have to agree to work for us for at least a year each, amounting to about 209 days worked for the year. There is time off in the summer during the low demand season but work is steady in the winter. We are short on labor so there will be plenty to keep you busy.

"We have quite a large Polish community in the area. We provide housing for couples and a bunk house for single men at reasonable rates, but you would have to reimburse us for your travel and initial living expenses. There

The Eagle's Nest

are churches, saloons and stores in the area. Most of the stores will advance you food and provisioning money against your wages. The pay is better than in Europe and it would give you a place to stay until the child is born, if you are interested."

"What is the pay?" Josef asked, intrigued at the mention of higher pay. Wages had been extremely low in Poland.

"It is normally based on a sliding scale tied to the current market price of coal. Right now as experienced workers, I can offer you $1.50 per day."

Josef's and Jan's eyes widened in surprise. That was $0.75 higher than in Poland!

The Polish clerk's lips tightened at the offer. He knew that was a low-ball wage for seasoned workers, but it would solve their immediate problem, and they would soon learn nothing came easy in this country either. All three frightened immigrants looked at each other.

"Could you give us a moment?" Jan asked.

"Certainly," the woman responded, as they stepped back from the desk.

"We don't have a way to contact Uncle Martin, if he is indeed on his way here, or even if he has been delayed," Jan said quietly in Polish.

"Surely he would have left word if he was delayed," Josef responded. "It seems more likely he didn't get our agenda. Staying in New York to find work doesn't appeal to me. We have no guarantee of work in the city. If we don't find work, they will send us back to Poland. I certainly don't want that after all we did to get here. Not that I am thrilled to work in coal fields again, but it will get us closer to the free land and allow us to stay in America."

Unaccustomed to city life, Jan didn't wish to stay in New York either. Yes, going to Pennsylvania would delay their schedule but Victor was in Pennsylvania. They would at least know someone there and they desperately needed the assistance. They had no extra money to feed themselves for more than a few days. With Suzanna being pregnant, he didn't dare endanger her or the baby's health.

"It only takes a couple of hours to get to Philadelphia by train, and the mine is not far from there. We could be there by tonight if we leave now," the woman added to encourage them.

Although not ideal, as neither men wanted to work deep beneath the earth in a coal mine, they nodded to each other. It would delay them but would solve their immediate problem. They could contact Martin about their change of plans once they were settled.

"Agreed," Jan decided, responding for all of them. Surely this was God's way of watching out for them in America.

New Territory

*O*nce settled on their wooden benches with their primary concerns settled, the trio watched the scenes of New York from the windows of the train. Cobbled streets and dirt roads were filled with the remnants of snow, and people manning pushcarts and carrying baskets overflowing with fruit, vegetables, poultry, fish, eggs, flowers, and one advertising old coats for 50 cents and ribbons for a penny. Horse drawn carriages and mule wagons forced pedestrians to jump out of their way. The Riskes were most intrigued to see black people, their first ever, handing out papers and mingling with every class of white people on the streets.

The Riske's astonished comments were noticed by a German-speaking gentlemen sitting near them. "They are gathering and promoting for the ratification of the 15th Amendment on April 30th, which will give Negroes the right to vote. Can't blame them. If I were in their shoes, I would be doing the same thing," he informed them. "New here?" he asked surmising their situation.

Josef nodded.

"You're lucky you made it across the ocean in one piece," the man confided. "One ship last season was hit by lightning that blew a hole about 2 feet wide on the port side of the vessel. It prostrated everyone on board and they had to scamper to even stay alive. But that is unusual, generally icebergs cause the most havoc. Despite that, this spring alone, over 44,000 immigrants have already reached our shores."

"That many? Dog's blood, I hope there is enough room for all of us," Josef commented.

"Oh, you'll find plenty of room, especially if you head west. The land goes on forever."

"Conditions are insufferable in most parts of Europe right now. We are from Poland and are only looking for a better life," Josef added.

"Well, you may or may not find it," the man responded honestly. "Injustice is still rampant here, too. One man can be sent to prison for stealing a turnip, while others are let free who have robbed communities of thousands of dollars and sent many families into beggary. A few days ago a man was convicted of rape, and sentenced to only 6 months imprisonment. If he had passed a bad shilling, he would probably get five years since it is a crime against property. We're working on it but justice is still not what it should be.

"See there," the man said pointing out the window, "those are gambling houses in the First Ward where illegal games of faro and roulette are played. Too many coppers are on the dole, when good money from those criminals could be used to remove refuse from the filthy streets. It's a disgrace for hard-working people to have to abide in such conditions.

"Families with too many children are forced to send them to work at a young age, too. In England they use youngsters as whelk gatherers. You know, the small spiral shellfish. The children gather them at ebb tide and are driven to barns near the coast and locked up together to wait until the next night or early morning ebb tide to do it again. Nasty business. Here they work in textile factories, separating wool, or what have you, from dawn to dusk."

Jan and Suzanna exchanged glances. They wanted their children to be free to live in healthy conditions and own their own property. They would do what they must to avert that kind of life for their children. They saw several fires against the early evening sky, a common site in all countries, from people not dousing embers adequately, or pouring oil on flames to get the wood or coal ignited faster. The primarily wooden structures of most cities burned quickly since indoor plumbing and water machines were few and far between the many occurrences.

"Of course, the further west you go, the more you have to deal with injuns. Ungodly creatures. They run around half naked and do unspeakable things to their enemies. But the cavalry will soon be rid of them," the stranger added.

"Have you been to Dakota Territory?" Jan eagerly asked.

"No, but they publish reports about all of the military campaigns in the newspapers. Evidently war with 26,000 Sioux, Cheyenne, and other northern tribes on the warpath is imminent over the government's failure to live up to its treaties with them. General Sherman has headquarters in Pembina, Minnesota and Custer has the 7th cavalry at Fort Hayes. You'll want to follow that in the newspapers if you are headed in that direction. We have newspapers printed in German and Irish, maybe even Polish, if you look. America is quite advanced that way."

Suzanna leaned against Jan for reassurance. Change was so stressful and she wasn't looking forward to dealing with savages. Trying to keep her faith in place, she snoozed as the star-filled night sky overtook the day as they headed toward their unexpected new future.

In the evening light, they couldn't see much when they switched trains in Philadelphia. It appeared to be a thriving metropolis, not quite as crowded as the New York area. When they arrived at Pottsville, 97 miles northwest of Philadelphia, they found it situated on the west bank of a river.

As they were escorted off the train by their benefactress she explained, "The land around here was originally granted to William Penn by Charles II. They say coal was discovered by a hunter named Necho Allen. Supposedly he fell asleep at the base of a mountain and awoke to the sight of a large fire. His campfire evidently had ignited an outcropping of coal. They eventually started mining the area and by 1795 an anthracite-fired iron furnace was established on the Schuylkill River," she said pointing to it.

"Pottsville began as a village in the Norwegian Township and has the oldest family beer brewery in the America. The biggest coal company here is the Philadelphia and Reading Coal and Iron Company. There is also a small textile industry that sells hand-sewn shirts to the local miners.

"Pottsville itself sits on seven hills and although there are no lakes within the city there are several water courses that flow throughout the city. We're headed to Minersville, which is just 4 miles west of here. The community is a mix of English, Irish, Welsh, German, Polish, and Slav miners. I think you'll feel right at home," she added.

When they arrived at Minersville she showed them to their quarters where they had a quick dinner of absconded bread from Castle Garden and water from the outdoor pump. After gathering his things, Josef promised to come by in the morning for him and Jan to meet with their new boss. On their first night alone from prying eyes in several weeks, Suzanna and Jan eagerly initiated their new bed then fell immediately to sleep from their exhausting day.

Indoctrination

The following day was Saturday, so they used their day to get settled in their quarters. Josef stowed his trunk with his tools and extra pants and shirt beneath his bunk in the dormitory, which held about 30 beds and several iron coal stoves. Suzanna and Jan's company housing was a small one-room shanty built of uninsulated, cheap wood planks. Suzanna unpacked the two remaining trunks as Jan and Josef left to meet with their new boss. The frozen snow-covered mine yard and streets were mingled with black soot and mud from the frequent traffic of the mules, wagons, and workers. They came across the company store, medical facilities, and administrative offices. Entering the Kaska Saloon, the bartender greeted them in Polish asking for their order.

"We're looking for Andres Bauer," Jan responded. The barkeep pointed to a burly, bearded man sitting at a table.

"*Ggyen-kuyeh*," Jan responded with 'thank you' in Polish.

"You must be the new help," Andres said, when they approached. "I appreciate you arriving on time. I run a tight crew. Please have a seat." He motioned for the barkeep to bring over a couple more tankards of beer.

"I hope you got settled in okay." Both men nodded in response.

"The mine manager allows us to house newly hired immigrants in their provided housing. You can change that at any time, if you want. Anton there," pointing to the bartender, "can tell you what other housing is available in the area. He will also loan you money, if you need it, or help you send money home if that is your desire. He keeps up on what is happening in the area and is an excellent source of information.

"So, this is how we operate here. Since you both have experience, you'll work underground from 7 a.m. until 2 or 3 in the afternoon. The mine we're working is several hundred feet, *lokiec*, below ground on the north face. I'm an independent miner and negotiate with the mine foreman for our work. Me and my crew hew the coal, and I'm paid for our produce on a piece-rate system. The foreman and I agree on a price to be paid for a wagon of coal, a ton of coal, or a length of coal seam mined. The younger boys on the crew, 14- to 18-year-olds, maintain the mine chamber and load coal into the carts for transport to the surface. They usually apprentice for a couple of years before they are old enough to work with the blasting powder.

"You'll see a lot of unskilled company men, who are paid by the hour, involved in transporting and sorting the coal. These haulers, mule drivers, and slate pickers, usually 12- to 13-years-old, work alongside the more skilled engineers, machinists, carpenters, and pump men to ensure that the mine is functioning properly.

"You'll want to keep your noses clean," Andres added. "The company keeps an extensive spy system and blacklist in order to root out unproductive or political troublemakers. If you do an honest day's work, you have nothing to worry about. My best workers earn $2.10 per day. If you work hard, maybe we can get you to that level.

"We have 37 furnaces in the LeHigh, Schuylkill, and Susquehamma regions, producing 270,000 tons of pig iron. We've had some heavy rains lately which caused a freshet—flood—that took out a dam and a coal boat. Bad luck there, as it will take a week to fix the dam. But we will continue to mine our area for now. I'll see you on Monday."

Both men shook hands with their new boss, then departed to pick up coal and food for the week. The company storekeeper agreed to extend them credit for their purchases of tea, sausages, flour, sugar, eggs, turnips and potatoes. They would celebrate their new-found luck with a good meal before they began their back-breaking labor.

Suzanna had made the small dwelling as comfortable as she could while the men were gone. Her wedding chest, their woven trunk, *pierzyny* (feather-filled comforter), and pillows cheered up the room. She had hung their crucifix over the bed and added the print of the Virgin Mary and child, and a traditional heron paper cutout pattern in Polish red on the plain walls. Her cooking implements were ensconced on a shelf over the fireplace and the table was covered with her new linens and dishes. She quickly scrambled eggs, potatoes and sausages for their first home-cooked meal in the new land. After dinner Jan composed letters to Martin, Victor, and their parents telling them of their new circumstances.

On Sunday, they walked to an Irish Catholic church in Pottsville, since no Polish church was available, and felt completely at home with the familiar Latin prayers and liturgy. They learned from the priest's interpreter of the church's rosary society, choral club, women's association, and youth organization, should they wish to participate. Walking through the town peering into stores, they soon learned that the majority of the commerce, at less expensive prices than in the company store, was centered in that town. It was a delightful respite from the stress they had all endured for the last several months. Through the grace of God, they were finally established in their new country and could earn some good wages, although they would be delayed one year at the coal mine. They felt truly blessed and thankful for being able to stay in the miracle of America.

Strike

Suzanna was busy the Tuesday before Ash Wednesday, *Pączki* Day, preparing for the traditional Polish feast. She fried fruit-filled doughnuts in order to use up the household sugar and fat before observation of the long fast of Lent. For the Polish people Easter was an important religious holiday as well as the beginning of the farmer's year. Consequently, Easter was celebrated with meals that included meats, butter molded into the shape of a lamb, and *pisanki*, elaborately decorated eggs, plus a good deal of drinking and merry-making.

During the Lent "Good Friday" religious ceremonies, they observed the Catholic Stations of the Cross, Christ's final days told in stages, in preparation for the resurrection of Christ from the dead as observed at Easter services. The church also put on a reenactment of His trials to entertain and inform the primarily uneducated church members.

On "Holy Saturday" prior to Easter Sunday on April 17, unlike the Polish, the Irish prepared a feast for the end of the month-long Lenten period. They placed fowls and pieces of bacon into a pot about 8 o'clock in the evening, but no one was allowed to taste it before midnight. At that time everyone cheered, clapped their hands and laughingly shouted "Out with the Lent!" They then proceeded to eat the tasty meal, then retired to rise early to see the sun dance in honor of Christ's resurrection on Easter morning. The Riskes were awakened and astonished at the commotion of their neighbors in the middle of the night.

At the Easter mass sermon, everyone was admonished by the residing priest that the "gods most worshipped were those of fashion, vice and drink." Jan and Josef exchanged weary grimaces when an Irish Polish-speaking acquaintance interpreted what the priest had said for them. It would be nice if they could afford such "gods."

They, however, had become accustomed, as they learned, to the relatively low pay for their jobs in the cold, pitch-black darkness in which they worked. Josef would set the blasting powder at the farthest end of their vein, then they would ignite the fuse, immediately running back up the tunnel to safety. When the blast blew, dust and falling rock flew everywhere and the cleanup began. The fallen rock was hauled out so that timbers could be placed for safe removal of the coal by pick axe and shovel. The work was dangerous because of loose falling rocks, misfired charges, and potential explosions of inadequately ventilated methane gas. They knew they were in danger from the buildup of methane when the rats started leaving an area.

The younger Polish workers on the coal breaker above ground fared little better. They were strictly supervised and worked three to four hours longer than the underground miners. Employers got the immigrants cheap, and frequently assigned them to the most dangerous and least profitable positions on the mine face. The other native workers were primarily indifferent to the Poles as they were known to be energetic, strong, and friendly when they had no provocation to be otherwise. Most Poles accepted the harsh working conditions in order to fulfill their dreams of returning to Poland with sufficient earnings to purchase farmland.

There were few amenities or women in Minersville as most of the men planned to return to their homeland, so Suzanna took in laundry for the coal miners to help the family build the nest egg they would need to supply their future home in Dakota Territory. Since coal mining was such filthy labor, the men went through many bars of lard-based homemade soap to get clean. Suzanna was busy from dawn to dusk making soap, cleaning and drying laundry, plus taking care of the household and making meals.

In general she followed the time-honored chore schedule of washing clothes on Monday, ironing them on Tuesday, sewing and mending on Wednesday, going to market with Jan on Thursday, cleaning house on Friday, baking on Saturday and attending church on Sunday. When the men returned from work each afternoon, they hauled coal or chopped wood, and sharpened their tools.

They did receive a letter from Julius saying his wife became sick after giving birth and the newborn passed away just when Martin was about to make the trip. They were glad they had found work, and although they were sad to have missed them, they decided given the circumstances they would wait for them to claim their land in Dakota Territory together. Resigned to their fate of waiting a year to claim their land, Jan, Josef, and Suzanna dreamed big dreams and made plans for their homesteads. They reimbursed Martin for the money he had lent them and became friends with the local saloon keeper.

The men met there to discuss the issues of the day and learn what they could about what they would need to homestead. For many, the west was too rough and isolated, and the would-be farmers returned to the "easier" labor of coal mining. But Jan's heart was set on owning his own property, cost free, and picked up a trail guide book from one of the failed farmers. He and Josef examined the guide religiously to memorize the route they would need to take. But it appeared that fate was still not finished with them.

By the end of April most of the collieries in the area were on strike for better wages. At an average of $10 a week for back-breaking labor of ten-hour work days, the strikers wanted the hours changed to 9 per day. The independent miners also wanted to directly pay their assistants, and not have them paid in saloons, as was the custom, so they couldn't be cheated.

The miners also complained about the different sizes of mine carts, the prices paid for such carts, and the unfair reduction of pay for carts deemed insufficiently loaded with coal. They also wanted abolishment of the sliding scale of pay based on the current price of coal. They demanded a fixed price be set that they could rely on, and that the price of blasting powder that they paid for be lowered from the current price of $1.65 per keg.

The collieries forced direct employees to use their company doctor and store, and used intimidation to stop workers from joining the union. When the miners went on strike anyway, striking workers were ordered to vacate their company homes.

In their free-time weekly wanderings, the Riskes discovered that the company housing they lived in was more expensive than many of the now empty local non-company offerings, as many of the miners expecting a long strike had moved on to distant collieries to find work. Since they were still under contract the Riskes found a two-bedroom house with a loft and a small backyard that they moved into. They immediately planted a garden with the seed they had brought from Poland, such vegetables as cabbage, carrots, cucumbers, potatoes, dill, and onions to offset their grocery expenses. They considered purchasing some chickens and a rooster to supplement their pantry, and sell their produce, since eggs were going for $0.25 a dozen, but decided they didn't want the added expense with the uncertainty of how long the strike would continue.

Suzanna was beginning to show her pregnancy, so she and Jan chose to stay at home during the strike. Jan began building a cradle for the baby as well as exploring the nearby countryside foraging for mushrooms, and hunting game with his treasured handmade flintlock breech, rear powder-and-ball loading musket. Bounties were being offered on fox, mink and polecat, so he kept a sharp eye out for them. He was fortunate one day and downed a deer, which was much larger than the type found in Europe. Jan also became quite the fisherman, learning all of the intricacies of fishing from the locals, and adding further to their empty larder.

Although they soon learned that the saloon was better patronized than the church on Sundays by both husbands and wives, Suzanna avoided that tradition. Pregnancy was considered a private state and women were to stay as secluded as possible. She busied herself with knitting baby clothes for the upcoming event. Jan, however frequented the Kaska Saloon, to ask the Polish bartender, Anton, about the Indians he had come across in his wanderings.

"Most of them still left around here are fairly peaceful and quite skilled at providing for themselves from either their farms or what nature provides. They're a queer lot. We see a few once in a while but they mostly stay away from the mining regions.

"Their wives rule the roost and wear pants as well as the men to prove it," he said. Jan's jaw dropped open in amazement.

"The devil take you!" Jan exclaimed in surprise. Anton nodded and continued.

"The women govern and allocate land to the families in the clan. They marry outside of their clans and the children belong to the mother. Newlyweds live with the bride's family, not the father's, where the bride's mother and sisters help raise the children."

"What an outlandish idea! Women don't have enough sense to rule. It says so in the Bible: Titus 2:5 'To be self-controlled, pure, working at home, kind, and submissive to their own husbands.' Their only role according to God is to please men and bear children. What do the Indian men do?"

"They cultivate the ground by slashing and burning, but the women grow and harvest primarily corn, squash, and beans. They plant maize and kidney beans near the corn to allow the beans to grow up the corn stalks. The big leaves of the squash cut down on the growth of weeds between the rows and help keep moisture in the soil. The women do most of the field work and processing of the food."

Jan exclaimed, "Well, Praise God for that!"

"The men build the houses, hunt anything that moves and even gather shellfish from the bays around here. And of course, they fight when offended or to protect their clan. All the males have their clan symbol—wolf, bear, turkey, or what have you—tattooed on their chests."

"The devil take you!" Jan said taking a large swallow of his beer, the thought of the pain involved with that making him cringe.

"They have an interesting way of hunting," Anton continued. "As a group they beat thigh bones on their hands to drive animals to the river, where they can be more easily killed. They also lasso and drown deer, as well as form a circle around prey and set the surrounding brush on fire to drive them toward the waiting hunters.

"Yes, they really are savages, and both men and women go bare-chested in hot weather. Since they buy their liquor here occasionally, I've seen quite a bit of them. In the winter they use beaver pelts or bear skins for cloaks. They dye deer hair scarlet, or use the iridescent feathers of turkeys and add it to their clothing. I've seen jewelry made of stone, shells, animal teeth, and claws. They are quite skilled at using what nature provides. Of course now they trade for cloth, decorating their clothing with ribbon patterns they design."

Jan shook his head, and couldn't get over the way they ran their societies, although he did appreciate their unique ideas of hunting game and using everything that God provided to survive. But no way would he ever let a woman govern him. What a heathenish, satanic idea. These people really did need to be civilized. When he later told Suzanna what he had learned, she was shocked but awed: imagine women controlling the households and having that much power.

Brotherly Love

Josef, feeling restless during the strike, contacted Victor and decided to travel to Philadelphia during his time off. Victor met him at the Reading Railroad station obviously delighted to see his former ship bunkmate. "Welcome to the 'City of Brotherly Love.' It is great to see you again. How are you?" Victor asked as they shook hands.

"I am grateful to be out in the fresh air, my friend," he replied with a smile, "but it is good to see you, too! What have you been doing with yourself?"

"I've been getting settled in and helping my sister. I also have been looking for work and may have an opportunity where my brother-in-law used to work. My sister introduced me to the owner of the *Philadelphia Gazette* newspaper and I plan on meeting with him next week about a possible opening. Other than that, I've been exploring the city. What is happening with the strike?"

"A lot of talk and many threats for engaging in the strike, but the miners are determined to get their grievances settled. Many miners have left, though, since they think it will be a long time before the strike is settled."

"That is rough luck, but at least I get to show you around this fine city!"

"The City of Brotherly Love?" Josef asked as they walked to Victor's carriage.

"Yes, '*Philadelphia maneto*' is Greek for 'let brotherly love endure.' The founder of the city was a Quaker, William Penn, who moved here to establish religious freedom on his property, but ended up starting a large community. As you can see," he said as he nodded at the bustling railroad station.

"Philadelphia has quite a history," he continued. "During the American Revolution the revolutionaries met here and signed the Declaration of Independence in 1776, and the Constitution. It was also one of the nation's capitals during the war." Victor pointed out the President's mansion where George

Washington and John Adams had lived during their presidencies. "Let's head to my sister's house and drop your things off, then I'll show you around."

Once en route, Josef was impressed by the variety of educational institutions they passed: the *Philadelphia Society for Promoting Agriculture*, the *Pennsylvania Society for the Encouragement of Manufactures and the Useful Arts*, and the *Academy of Natural Sciences*. He thought the schools were quite an accomplishment for a relatively new country extracted from the wilderness.

It didn't take them long to arrive at a two-story home with a large garden area, stable, and carriage house. At Josef's surprised look, Victor explained, "Before being drafted, my brother-in-law worked at a newspaper that was previously owned by Benjamin Franklin. He was doing quite well but since his demise, my sister takes in boarders to feed the family."

After exchanging greetings with Victor's sister, they continued their tour of the city. They encountered a wide variety of sailors and stevedores loudly pursuing their duties along the Delaware and Schuylkill river piers and business canals.

They passed textile businesses that sold calicos, muslins, fine flannels, crinoline, hoop skirts, hosiery, dress trimmings, leather gloves, handkerchiefs, black grosgrain, silks, velvets, ribbons, satin, yarn and knit goods—all listed as "prices lower than ever." There were businesses that sold fancy soaps and toilet articles, nightcaps, hats, feathers, fur and fur trimmings, capes, cuffs, and collars. There were book binderies, confectionaries, toys, and fruit stores.

Meat markets offered pork, mutton, and beef wagon runs every day except Sunday. Barber saloons advertised the best shaving and hair dressings while eating houses offered a warm meal of game or fish at any hour of the day for $0.10.

"I want you to see this museum in particular," Victor said as they stopped at the *Franklin Institute*. "I've been doing some research here so I can impress the owner of the newspaper when I talk to him. Having learned English from my mother was a big help but my sister said the owner is a huge admirer of Franklin, so I figured it couldn't hurt to learn more about him."

Josef nodded, impressed. Victor certainly was smart to do what he needed to advance his position in life.

The science museum was devoted to the investigation of the mechanical arts, such as steam engines and water power. There they saw replicas of some of Franklin's inventions. One was the Franklin stove, which was a metal-lined fireplace for cooking and heating that produced more heat and less smoke than an ordinary open fireplace. It had a hollow baffle (ductwork) to transfer heat from the fire to a room's air before the smoke went up the chimney.

"Franklin never patented any of his inventions," Victor mentioned as they looked at the displays of Franklin's creations which included his research theories regarding electricity, his lightning rod, and bifocal eyeglasses. "He believed in improving human efficiency and welfare, and contributed research into population studies, including slave demographics. Toward the end of his life, he freed his own slaves and was a prominent abolitionist.

"The man was amazing. He even analyzed ocean currents and actually named the Gulf Stream, which eventually cut travel time across the Atlantic by two weeks."

"Dog's blood, how did he accomplish all of this?" Josef asked, as they left the building.

"It's hard to say," Victor responded. "He was one of the founding fathers of America, former President of Philadelphia, and an ambassador for America in England and France. I do know he lived by a strict moral code and made most of his wealth by publishing *Poor Richard's Almanac*."

Even Josef had heard of *Poor Richard's Almanac*, and knew several of the adages used for many occasions, such as, "A penny saved is two pence dear" and "Fish and visitors stink in three days."

"It's about time for some refreshments," Victor said as he pulled up to a building entitled *The Tun Tavern*. The three-story wooden edifice had a railed, wide porch and was a hive of activity. Victor was obviously known in the bar as several clients greeted him when he entered. "They make the best scrapple here," he commented to Josef.

"Scrapple?"

"It's a fried mush loaf of pork scraps combined with cornmeal and wheat flour, or often buckwheat flour, and spices. You'll love it."

After they sat down, ordered tankards and the house special, Victor pointed out a framed document written in German on the wall next to Josef. "That is one of the reasons, I have come to admire Franklin," he said.

Josef read the document, which was an extensive list of the virtues Franklin had lived by as stated in his autobiography, such as temperance, silence, order, resolution, frugality, industry, sincerity, justice, moderation, cleanliness, tranquility, chastity, and humility.

"That's quite an admirable list but I wonder why anyone would hang it here?" Josef asked.

"This tavern is where he organized the Pennsylvania Militia to recruit soldiers to go to war against the Indian tribes who were massacring the colonists. They still meet here, and I have joined their ranks," Victor responded, grinning at his friend's astounded face, then became serious as he further explained.

"During the civil war, the Pennsylvania Brigade lost more than 3,500 men at Gettysburg. Losing my brother-in-law hit me hard. He was a great help to our family during tough times in Germany, and a sort of mentor to me before he came to America. I feel it is my duty, in his honor, to protect this new country from the Indian raids that still occur here. So I joined up," he explained. "I know Jan said a member of your family perished at Gettysburg, too. You might want to think about joining yourself."

For the rest of his leave, Josef and Victor caroused as young men will and frequently met with the members of the Pennsylvania militia. Josef made many new friends there and was thrilled to be on a horse again in their company. He *would* think about joining the militia.

Challenges

*J*an was happy to be back at work after the strike was resolved. Every penny he made brought him closer to his goal of owning his own land, but the news from the west was not good. Not all of the Indians were on reservations and the free ones were frequently on the warpath.

In a Wyoming gold mining area, a man was killed by a group of 25 Indians. Five other bodies were found horribly mutilated, with four more people still missing and presumed dead. Not far from there a stage coach with five passengers was past due and was believed to have been captured by 75 to 100 Sioux Indians.

At Fort Sully, Dakota, 800 Sioux and other Indians were camped near the Cheyenne Indian agency. They wanted arms and ammunition, and claimed they planned to drive all the miners from the Muscle Shell and Yellow Stone Rivers, and from the Wind River country for taking all of their gold from the region. Many employees there had left in fright due to the Sioux performing war dances and waving scalps of white men and women they had killed in front of the fort.

Jan frowned at the newspaper articles. That was definitely not good. *How could he protect Suzanna against such wild opponents?*

As Jan read on, he discovered that a recent raid on the Union Pacific Railroad by the Dakota Nations of Indians was caused by many factors. The Indians were initially promised 40 years of free roaming, including the whole Platt Valley teeming with buffalo in 1861, but the American Senate reversed their decision and reduced the time to ten years. Some tribes accepted the change but others, including Chief Red Cloud's, Chief Single Horn's, and other tribes didn't. Up until just after they arrived in America, military posts were set up along the base of some place called the Big Horn Mountains, evidently the Indians last, best hunting grounds. This infuriated the free tribes and Red Cloud demanded the forts be closed, and came in to sign the treaty only after the government complied with his request.

Turmoil further ensued, Jan learned, when the Indians were asked to live on agricultural reservations and most refused. General Sherman reported it would take 20,000 men, one-half mounted, to protect the railroad line that was being built through that part of the frontier. General Terry in the Department of Dakota said he would need the same amount of help to protect his region.

The Indians felt justified in their refusal to live on reservations due to the 16th article of the treaty they had signed which gave them the right to roam and hunt on that land until they agreed to something different. The 10th article of the treaty to send them clothing and $10 of supplies each, also had not been honored, nor the ability to dispose of their 'products of the chase' at fair rates. Because of these broken promises by the government, the Indians vowed to enter into war on the entire American frontier.

That was certainly not good news, Jan thought, as he pulled out his trail guide to see if these places were anywhere near Dakota Territory where they planned to move. Luckily it seemed to be further west, but still too close for comfort.

In his readings Jan learned that there were at least 12,000 roaming Indians and it was believed that in a few years the majority of all the free-range game would be gone. The Indians would have no choice but to settle down to survive in a manner to which they were not accustomed. John Sanborn, the Commissioner to the Indians, recommended the government make peace with the Indians, otherwise it could cost America somewhere near $50,000,000 to police the plains. The government responded by sending General Sheridan to the Dakota area with 4,000 troops to stop the conflicts.

Well, at least the Americans were going to fight for what they wanted, Jan thought, *but where would that leave them and their plans for farming next year when their contract was completed?*

There were many predictions of spring wars since the tribes considered the treaties binding and didn't understand the mechanics of the American government—that the treaties had to be ratified by the Senate, nor that Congress needed to legislate Indian policy. Jan learned that the demands on the government were enormous. In one article he was surprised to learn that the Cheyenne Agency alone was requesting one month supplies of sugar, coffee and bacon for 9,500 Indians. *That was a lot of people to care for. Could the Americans afford it? Had he made the right decision to come to this land?*

Eventually the Piegan massacre, Big Horn fort expedition and the government's failure to meet its obligations were considered to be the cause of all of the tension. The Piegan massacre of 53 Indian women and children, with another 140 women and children captured then released, Jan discovered, had been considered a catastrophe. Coronel Baker, the head of that expedition, testified that he burned that camp to the ground since its inhabitants had been stricken with smallpox—but he had left the survivors without winter supplies or help during below zero temperatures. *Such inconsideration, heartlessness, and incompetence!* Jan thought.

He was relieved to learn that most of the Indian tragedies were occurring primarily on the frontier, not in the established territories. This was because America's system of giving public lands to anyone did not permit the communities on the frontiers to establish governing bodies as was done under the territorial system. Those who ventured into the frontier had to protect their lives and property with their own ingenuity. They, of course, wanted the free Indians to be collected and taught civilized life by the American government.

Another part of the problem was that there were 800,000 unemployed Civil War soldiers who had headed to the northwest after the war and many were causing havoc wherever they went on the frontier. The Quaker agents sent to help could do nothing against the white ruffians nor the hostile Indians. So the Indians were not all to blame. In Omaha, Nebraska, and Arizona, Mexicans attacked the railroads and stole stock. Even white men, disguised as Indians, were captured for crimes near Fort Hayes.

After reading the news, and talking the situation over with Anton, Jan discussed what he had learned with Suzanna. She was terrified of the newspaper reports. "What are we going to do? How can we move to such an area where we will always be in fear for our lives?"

The Eagle's Nest

Jan tried to calm her down. "It is not all bad news," he said. "In the area where Uncle Martin has been talking about, the Sioux are no longer a threat. According to what Anton heard from his customers, they moved out of the region in 1868. The area just north of where we are headed is owned by the French in Canada. They sold Fort Gary, Winnipeg to the Hudson Bay Trading Company. The Indians there are called *Metis*, who converted to the Catholic religion and are considered to be what he called 'priest-ridden.' Although I consider that a degrading term, the fact that the Indians are now Catholic is a good thing. Many are half-breeds who are honest and friendly with whites. Their interbreeding seems to have resulted from losing quite a few of their people to a smallpox epidemic that decimated many of their tribes."

Suzanna shuddered at that revelation. She had seen victims of smallpox, with their swelling bodies accompanied by foul odors and delirium during the illness, and later, the disfigurement of the few survivors.

"Anton said the Metis generally traded fur with the forts, but as the white settlers increased, in order to protect their business interests, the fur traders incited the Metis to revolt by tearing down settler fences, driving off their livestock and burning their crops."

Suzanna was appalled by the greediness and callousness of it all. "God have mercy!" she exclaimed.

"My point is," Jan continued, "the remaining Metis are Christians and peaceful in that area of Dakota Territory. Trust me, Suzanna, I will not take our family anywhere unsafe, nor will we go until we have enough money saved to provide a good home for our family," he added as he patted her expanding belly.

Suzanna smiled her gratitude at her husband. She did trust him but despite that, because of the horror of the revelations, that night she again dreamed nightmares.

Winter's Gift

The total eclipse of the sun on December 22 worried Suzanna since she believed no good ever came when Satan, demonstrating his power, made the sun disappear. Being about to give birth any time soon, she prayed special prayers to the Blessed Virgin and decided to rid herself of her fears by making Christmas especially cheerful with a traditional Polish celebration. From doing the laundry for so many single Poles, Suzanna had come to know quite a few of them. Jan was unnerved that unmarried men were visiting his wife, as it was totally improper, but he knew they needed the money and had grudgingly allowed it.

On December 6, she had been surprised that many "St. Nicklaus's" brought her almond cookies, apples, honey, and holy pictures of the nativity. In gratitude for their thoughtfulness, she and Jan invited the homesick bachelors to celebrate Christmas Eve with them. When they all arrived, the *wigilia*, Christmas Eve dinner, began when the first star of the evening appeared. The dinner was served upon a quickly constructed plank-table covered with a white tablecloth from her trousseau under which straw had been placed. The meal consisted of 12 meatless courses, representing one for each apostle. They made certain there was an even number of people at the table to ensure good health, in addition to one empty seat left open for any stranger who might drop by.

The feast began with the breaking of the blessed Christmas wafer, the *oplatek,* and the exchange of good wishes from everyone present. Suzanna served mushroom soup, apple and potato pancakes, fish, *gołabki* (cabbage rolls), *pierogi* (a filled dumpling), deviled eggs, sauerkraut, beets, nuts, fruitcake, and a poppy seed torte for dessert. Everyone present followed the tradition of tasting every entree to insure good luck in the coming year. Suzanna served their guests then ate herself, as was the Polish custom to honor the dominant position of guests and men in their communities. After the meal, the men gathered around the fire to sing carols and drink vodka, as well as to discuss what was happening in their world.

"That was some explosion near Titusville the other day, wasn't it? They say that wagon was filled with cans carrying 300 pounds of nitroglycerine meant for excavating a coal face. The driver, wagon and team were blown to bits when it exploded. It apparently blew a huge hole in the road, shattering all the fences and trees along it into pieces. They say a barn within range was actually blown to fragments by the force of it, and many nearby houses were twisted out of shape. Even the butt end of the driver's whip traveled a full 1/4 mile and knocked a woman unconscious. Some said it felt like an earthquake extending for several miles around," one man commented.

"At least only one person was killed this time," another guest added. The miners were fully aware of the dangers of working in mines. They frequently heard weekly or monthly reports of explosions, fires, or cave-ins caused by human error or nature.

"So are you still planning to head out west?" one guest asked Jan, to change the subject, all too aware of many of the men's own anxieties such events caused.

"Oh, yes, most definitely. There is free land in Dakota territory that I plan to claim once our contract is up."

"Me, I'm going home as soon as I can save more money," one devout bachelor responded. "There aren't enough good Catholic Polish women like your wife around here, and I have to admit, I miss my country. But when I get back, I will marry my sweetheart, live like a prince and have many children," he said with a big smile added to temper his desires. "I, of course, want to have enough to bury me properly in hallowed ground when I pass back into the Lord's hands."

Most nodded in agreement. All wanted love and the pleasures of life but it was almost a sacred duty to be buried in a church cemetery. Money and coffins were always arranged in advance for those purposes if at all possible. Most of the immigrants had brought a small amount of Polish soil to be buried with them should they perish in the new land.

"Pray God, I hope the wars are over by then. My family reports the French and Prussians are still fighting, causing havoc and destruction, and stripping the land of needed food in the villages. The Russians are still oppressing and conscripting our young brethren. They said that many are starving and near death's door since there were not enough young bodies to plant or attend to the small harvests. I send back as much money as I can to help out, of course. But when I die, I'd rather it be in Poland, and not by the hands of some wild savage who scalps you."

"They are not all bad," Jan responded optimistically. "My Uncle Martin said the tribe in north eastern Dakota Territory are a peaceful tribe, called the Chippewa or Ojibwa. He talks to the steamboat crews and says he has heard tales that the earth there has a dark black, rich soil for miles around waiting to be planted, with herds of elk, deer, moose, bear and wolf to harvest and provide fur trade. Europe is too crowded for me. I want some open country to live on in peace."

"If we can find peace there. Even the Delaware tribe north of here is still raiding isolated homeowners or travelers," Josef commented with obvious concern. "Victor has written of some of their scrimmages. He says they are a wild, relentless enemy."

Because of her fears of the Indians and the dangers of the mines, Suzanna uncharacteristically joined the conversation with the men to change the subject to a more pleasant topic than death.

"Will we see you at the 'caroling of the manger'?" she asked one guest.

Jan looked at her in shock. Polish women never questioned nor interrupted men in their discussions. Men ruled the household and women were subject to their rule, according to 1 Timothy 2:11-15—"Let a woman learn quietly with all submissiveness. I do not permit a woman to teach or to exercise authority over a man; rather, she is to remain quiet. For Adam was formed first, then Eve; and Adam was not deceived, but the woman was deceived and became a transgressor. Yet she will be saved through childbearing—if they continue in faith and love and holiness, with self-control." Jan silently prayed that her breaking of God's law would be forgiven with the upcoming birth.

"Most definitely. They will be off-key without my melodious voice," he replied. "How about you?"

In Poland, between Christmas Eve and Epiphany (also known as 'The Three Kings'), a custom is celebrated in which carolers carry a handcrafted manger to each of their neighboring households singing their hearts out despite the cold weather each January 6. Suzanna planned to prepare a large batch of *babka* (coffeecake) to reward any carolers who came their way.

"It will depend on the situation," Jan nodded in his wife's direction, referring to the common knowledge of either mother or child dying during the birth process, or shortly thereafter. Jan refused to believe God would curse them that way, however, and continued, "But we should be able to participate in the close of the Christmas season on Candlemas Day, February 2. We'll need the God-blessed candles from the church to protect my home and family from sickness or bad fortune this year in particular."

The Riskes had taken their foreman's advice and used the company doctor for Suzanna's examinations. No midwife could be found close enough to help with the delivery. Although embarrassing for Suzanna, and obviously uncomfortable for a jealous Jan to have another man touch his wife, the male doctor was the only option. Their foreman's wife had agreed to stop by for proprieties sake when the time came to help with the delivery.

Dark gray mushroom topped clouds broke the overcast sky against the dark green of the mountain pine trees in the distance. Just after the first of 1871 when the men were hard at work in the frigid air below ground, Suzanna had a lower backache. The difficult laundry work of scrubbing and boiling dirty, coal-stained miner clothes, after porting the water in from the outdoor pump, had left her feeling tired today. Lately she had been full of the well-known pre-birth energy God provides women to ensure that the household is impeccably prepared for the arrival of new life, so her loss of energy surprised her. When pains began weaving from the small of her back to the front of her abdomen, she was startled from her normal mindless chore stupor. When her water broke and a stream of warm liquid flowed down her legs, she knew she was in labor and it was time to contact the doctor. She immediately asked her neighbor to send her eldest son to notify the doctor that the birth was imminent.

By the time Jan arrived home from the mines, Suzanna was in full labor, unbearable pain and fully dilated. As the doctor urged Suzanna to push, Jan reviewed the teachings from Genesis 3:16 to alleviate any doubts that such pain was God-given and not the Devil's work—"To the woman he said, 'I will surely multiply your pain in childbearing; in pain you shall bring forth children. Your desire shall be for your husband, and he shall rule over you."

August Riske, named after Jan's cousin who had died at the Battle of Gettysburg, emerged into the cold hands of the doctor minutes later and protested his new situation with a piteous yelp of shock on January 5. Jan and Suzanna were delighted to have a son. The next day the carolers were thrilled to receive a glimpse of the newborn but Jan refused their request to place the baby in the manger to travel throughout the remainder of the village.

August was baptized two weeks later on a Sunday after mass with Josef as his godfather and their foreman's wife as the godmother. The vital ceremony was performed to ensure his eventual entry into the heavenly realms and included a purification rite for Suzanna as well. After the christening, a feast supplied primarily by the guests was held at the Riske's home where the newborn was presented with gifts of money, linens and baby caps. Much vodka was consumed by all but Suzanna, and the event was considered a wonderful success. Life had suddenly become much more rewarding and busy with the birth of their son.

Disaster

Jan left the house happy that day. They were getting close to the end of their contract date, and tulips and daffodils were adding cheerful color to the sunny spring day. August, Jan's pride and joy, was growing and soon they would be able to leave to meet his uncle and cousins to go to Dakota Territory. Life was good.

On his walk to work he passed miners on their way to a new surface rock face where they would cut, blast, and remove rock to reach the coal in that area. The already established underground mine was where he and Josef worked.

Jan passed the breaker boy station, where the children and some elderly coal miners were already hard at work separating impurities such as rock, slate, or clay from the bituminous coal by hand from a coal breaker. The coal breaker broke the coal into pieces and sorted these pieces into uniform sizes.

Lumps of coal were placed on screens of cast iron and "breakers" would hammer the coal until it was small enough to fall through the holes. A second screen caught the coal, and was shaken to remove the worthless smaller lumps. This broken coal was considered higher quality since the even sizes ignited more quickly, and needed less tending, once past the ignition point.

The removal of refuse from the coal was done by hand for ten hours a day, six days a week. The boys would sit perched over the chutes and conveyor belts, handpicking debris out of the stream of coal passing by them. The boys would often cut their fingers on the sharp refuse slate—but continued working despite their injuries.

The rapidly moving conveyor belts and gears were a danger to limbs or fingers if the picker wasn't careful. The boys also could be ensnared by the rush of coal down the chute, and be crushed to death, or smothered, before they could be rescued. The dust of the dry coal itself caused asthma and black lung disease among the workers. When the coal was rinsed with water to help remove clinging dirt, sulfuric acid was created, which also burned the hands of the boys. Jan nodded to any of the boys who dared to look up from their hazardous work.

Jan passed hewers who were hurrying to their stations to release the bituminous coal with a pickaxe. In the old country Josef had apprenticed his way up from a breaker boy, to the pit itself to learn the skills of a putter, transporting material around the mine in wagons. Only afterward did he learn the skills of a hewer. As a hewer, he had reported to the mine foreman and thus was respected by the other miners.

Here, however, Josef and Jan worked with anthracite coal. Anthracite coal underwent little processing before being sold. They would use a sledgehammer to break large pieces of coal, then use a rake with teeth set two inches apart to collect the broken coal. This coal was shoveled into sacks that could be carried out of the mine, or loaded onto a pack animal if the tunnel they were in was large enough.

The variety of workers was quite specific. Drillers worked a rock drill to bore holes for placing dynamite or other explosives. Loaders shoveled coal into the mining carts at the face. Barrow-men transported the broken coal from the mine entrance in wheelbarrows. Timber workers installed wooden support structures to create the walls and ceilings of the underground mines. Brakemen operated the winding mechanics of the underground entry shaft.

Each miner owned a mandrill, a small pick for use in confined spaces. They also had coal shovels with a wide, flat blade and steeply turned sides to better handle the coal. The tools had a hole in their handles so they could be latched to a locked tool ring, or they were secured in a chest to prevent thievery.

Jan entered onto the shaft platform and descended along with a group of other miners. Once reaching the bottom, he headed toward the south gangway where he entered the dinner shanty and left his lunch pail. He met Josef in their tunnel and they worked hard for several hours clearing coal from a recent blast area, when the earth suddenly shook and rocks began tumbling around them. Their pit pony reared, bolted and ran right into Jan, breaking his right arm.

The Eagle's Nest

Josef was stunned by the falling debris but immediately grabbed Jan and helped him towards the mine entrance following the path of the panicked horse. It was early afternoon but that wasn't evident by the smoke that was beginning to billow around them.

When they arrived near the entry shaft they learned that it was on fire and a group of men were in the process of building a barricade across the entrance to the south gangway. After the barricade was finished the group sat down, Jan clutching his shattered arm and groaning in agony. Some men despaired as the fire consumed their only route of escape. All were anxious, hoping they would see the sky and their loved ones again.

❀

Outside the mine, no water was closer than a mile away, so teams of wagons were hurriedly bringing water in barrels to the disaster area. Lines of men formed to hand pails of water from one to another to throw it into the mouth of the shaft.

By 7 p.m. the red-hot materials surrounding the entrance had cooled enough to let a dog down into the shaft on a rope for a couple of minutes. After the dog was pulled out alive, the mine supervisor was let down to about 80 feet before he had to be lifted out again. The rescue team decided to allow two men down to 30 feet to clear the burned timber and build a partition to construct a funnel for air to enter and leave the mine. Once they did, dense smoke emerged from the shaft and a strong current of air began descending down the opening. Hopefully the fresh air would reach those still alive.

It was slow work clearing the debris but finally near midnight three men volunteered to enter the burning mine to look for their comrades. When they reached the bottom, they discovered several bodies, horses, and mules near the gangways. Further down the tunnel they encountered a barricade with words written on it saying, "We are in here."

All of the miners imprisoned behind the barricade knew technically what the process of their death would be. The combustion of all carbon-containing fuels, such as coal, wood and organic matter produces carbon dioxide and water.

High amounts of carbon dioxide, also known as blackdamp, sinks and collects near the floor, making people drowsy, dizzy, and have a headache. Unconsciousness could occur within a few minutes to an hour.

Josef watched as many of his fellow comrades developed flushed, pink skin and breathed rapidly to alleviate their shortness of breath. Several men's muscles were twitching and had uncontrollable flapping of their hands as the asphyxiate gas and the lack of oxygen began affecting them. Some became confused and wondered why they were barricaded in, when they should be trying to get out. Several weaved around as if drunk while others became lethargic and slumped to the ground, heads in their hands. They sang hymns for a while, praying to God for his mercy, but as time passed many of them succumbed to panic, became emotionally irrational then died due to cardiac arrest. It was a horrific scene to watch.

Josef forced Jan to stand and walk as much as possible to reach the cleaner air near the top of the tunnel but both wept as their co-workers passed on one by one. They could die of suffocation at any moment. As the hours passed, Josef cursed while Jan prayed in their entombment.

The rescue crew lifted the bodies as they were discovered up through the shaft. When the barricade was finally breached, men were found lying insensible, some still alive, but most dead. It took until almost noon the next day to bring them all out. Only 16 of the 35 miners escaped the mine shaft alive.

Recovery

Suzanna had been overwrought and frightened when she learned of the fire and had hurried with August to the site. When she couldn't find evidence of either Jan or Josef, she despaired for their lives, and dropped to her knees and began praying to every saint she knew for mercy for her family. August fell asleep in her arms but she did not leave the site until they were rescued. Praising God, she hurried to their sides when they emerged, pushing people out of her way to get to them. Weeping with joy that they still lived, it had been a ghastly experience for everyone. After both men were examined by the doctor and Jan's arm was set, they had been released to go home. She had nervously fretted over both of them since then, making sure they were comfortable and not in undue pain.

The Minersville funeral was held the following week, with all stores and businesses closed, many draped with mourning flags. Several thousand people attended the funeral held at an orchard in view of the disaster area where the coffins were lined up. There were few dry eyes in sight as the cries of surviving wives and children permeated the chosen burial site.

An inquest had been begun by the authorities and it was judged that the men had died from foul air and the effects of "carbonic acid gas." The cause of the fire was determined to be friction created by an inadequately greased ventilation fan near the top of the entrance shaft of the mine. They had been experimenting on the fan to increase the revolution rate when the tragedy occurred. That, however, did not alleviate the destruction of lives.

There was no compensation for the dead men, their relatives, nor those miners who had survived. The widowed women and orphaned children would be forced to move out of the company housing and to find other means of making a living. The sick still under contract were tended by the company doctor but were incurring large debts, or using their meager savings to pay for his services.

The Riskes did attend the funeral with some difficulty as Josef and Jan were still recovering from their ordeal, but despite their weaknesses, hobbled to the funeral along with everyone else. When they returned home, they discussed their options. Though still coughing heavily with muscular aches and pains, Josef was relatively unscathed by the fire, but Jan would be unable to work for several months as his arm healed. All were distressed by the situation.

"How will we pay the rent until I can work again? Even using my savings, it is not enough to feed us," Jan surmised. The constant pain he was in was making him peevish, and drinking vodka to ease his agony and survivor remorse wasn't helping his attitude.

Suzanna shook her head as she tended to August. Someone must have cursed them with the evil eye to cause this to happen to them. She would have to pray special prayers to her patron saint to alleviate the dangers they now faced. She had no idea how much money Jan earned, as most wives didn't, but she knew her laundry earnings would not cover the rent. Nor were women allowed to work in the mines, which she thought was unfair, for she believed she was as nimble and strong as many men.

"I can help out," Josef quickly replied.

"No, I can't let you do that. You need the means to live, too."

"Not if I moved in with you," Josef responded.

In Minersville, the general lack of company housing made a boardinghouse system rampant in the area. Nearly half of the Poles they knew had taken in boarders to survive.

"I can bunk in August's room instead of living in the bachelor dormitory. The food is better here anyway," he said with a smile.

"Won't you miss your comrades?"

"I see them every day at work or the saloon. I'd much prefer being able to see my nephew daily and teach him how to drive his father crazy," Josef responded with a grin. "Remember the trouble we used to get into when we were kids?"

"Yes, yes. I particularly remember us burning down the outhouse," Jan laughed. "My backside hurt for days after that beating! I never knew anyone who could grab a switch faster than my father."

After thinking a while he told Josef that he would be welcome to live with them. Family was important. If they were in opposite positions, he would do the same for Josef and they sincerely needed the help until he healed. His arm wasn't just broken, but fractured in several places, which would take longer to mend. *Praise God for loving family*, he thought.

Josef moved his gear over the next day and thus began a new phase of their lives. When Josef returned home from work each day, he would help Suzanna as much as possible with her and Jan's normal chores. He played with August and entertained Jan with stories of what was happening at work—the rebuilding of the destroyed shaft and tunnels—to relieve him of his convalescent boredom. They became a close knit group and Suzanna sincerely appreciated his help when she learned what a truly kind man was hidden beneath his quiet character.

Even with Josef's help with the rent, their doctor bills forced them to extend their stay in the coal mines to pay their debts when Jan healed enough to rejoin the workforce. Jan enjoyed Josef's company and noticed how Suzanna became more cheerful when he was around. He often thought of the Polish proverb, "*Wszędzie dobrze ale w domu najlepiej*," meaning "everywhere is fine but best at home."

When they celebrated August's first birthday, they set him on the floor surrounded by a vodka glass, a book, a rosary and a banknote. When he reached for the banknote first, Suzanna laughed.

"Just like his father, he will try to be a person of wealth," she said. "Thank the Blessed Virgin for your help, Josef. We couldn't have done it without you. Hopefully August will be successful so that we can live like nobility. I'm glad he didn't choose to be a toper, scholar or priest. We don't need a drunk, although a priest would be grand. We could certainly use his intercession with God right now, but I do want grandchildren."

Jan frowned at her comment. Since they were so overburdened with debt, he felt that Suzanna didn't respect him or his abilities to provide for his family any more. His recovery had been a long one and he was just now regaining his full strength and vitality.

Josef smiled at Suzanna and Jan enviously, "Surely a beautiful woman like you will certainly have more children before grandchildren! Once this cousin of mine remembers how to do it, that is," he said teasingly.

Jan laughed along with both of them but Josef's comment and admiring glance at Suzanna gave him pause. Matthew 5:28 said, "But I say to you that everyone who looks at a woman with lustful intent has already committed adultery with her in his heart." Although he loved Josef and didn't believe he would ever betray his trust, it wasn't healthy for Josef not to have a woman of his own. And Josef was right—it was time to have another child. August needed a brother or sister to play with. He would have to take care of that.

Learning the Land

With Jan back to work and healthy again, other than having developed a tendency toward claustrophobia, Josef was getting restless. He needed an outlet for his free time. The next break they had in work, he went to visit Victor again and was convinced to join the Pennsylvania militia. He had completed his mining contract and could leave any time he felt so inclined. The close quarters and Jan's renewed interest in his wife was beginning to grate on his nerves. With no outlet for his pent-up energy, he knew he would go insane unless he made a change in his life. He would travel to Dakota Territory with Jan when they were ready to move on, but now he needed a change of pace, something that would remove him from the hell's cavern in which he worked.

He felt he was too young to be living his life in a hole in the ground, away from the beauty and life-sustaining aspects of nature. Nor did he want to die underground either, as was a daily danger of which he must be constantly aware. Life was so unpredictable—one misplaced spark, could be the end of him. Not that there weren't many other avenues to death—you could even be killed crossing the street.

Just the other day a team of horses pulling a wagon filled with beer was scared by a passing train. The horses dashed down the street, flinging the driver off at a corner, breaking his leg. A gentleman and a lady were then hit by the frightened team as it raced through a crosswalk. The woman was killed and the man's arm was broken by the deadly encounter. But he would rather take his chances where he couldn't be as completely trapped, at the mercy of only one escape route. After the last explosion, he had grown anxious each time he had to enter the stifling blackness of the mineshaft. Life was too uncertain to spend it almost entirely in the deep recesses of the earth.

He had to admit part of the attraction of joining the militia was so he could be with his beloved horses again. He knew horses. He knew how they thought and why they acted the way they did. He missed the joy of riding them at full speed to a destination—any destination. He decided he would start out simple and volunteer during the off times at the mine. Then he could still save what he would need to start his own stable, and there were certainly more women in Philadelphia than in Minersville. It also would be good to get to know more about his potential, future adversaries—the red men.

One day while tightening the leaking water pump pipe outdoors after work, Josef heard someone giggle, and glanced toward where Suzanna was attaching a wet shirt to the strung rope with a clothespin from her clothespin bag. Beyond the line of flapping clothes, Josef caught a glimpse of two young Indian women seated in the grass, dressed in calf-length tightly woven, straight-necked, fringed dresses. They wore moccasins on their feet and one of them had her legs folded neatly beneath her.

"Do you think he can see us?" one of them asked in English. The other looked his way and smiled broadly. She had high cheekbones and her smile seemed to light up the sky, she beamed so brightly. The first had long, braided hair while the sunbeam-girl had hers pulled back from her face, but hanging down free to her waist in the back.

Startled by the sight, when he could once again see beyond the hanging clothes, they were gone. "Who was that?" he asked Suzanna.

"The Indian girls? They live with the widow in the next house over. They were orphaned when young and raised by a local Christian ministry, where they learned German and the English language. When Anna lost her husband during the war several years ago, she took them in to help run her boarding house and raise her children. The girls have evidently been a big help to her," Suzanna replied.

Orphaned! What a horrible thought. Josef didn't know what he would do without family around him. Unlike most young men, he did regularly stay in contact with his relatives in Poland and sent money home frequently. The girls must be as lonely as he had felt at times, like the lone survivor of a shipwreck, without his brothers and sisters around.

"Anna's boarding house is always full, so she must run a good household," Suzanna continued. "She is a kind-hearted soul who speaks German and teaches English to those who want to learn. She holds classes every Sunday afternoon, if you are interested."

Josef nodded his head at Suzanna, "That might be a good idea—to learn English while we're here. There aren't always Poles or Germans around with whom we can communicate, and who knows what we may find in Dakota Territory. Primarily English speakers, I would guess." They had all picked up a few English words, but not many.

"I don't know if I could spare the time with August walking and getting into so much mischief," Suzanna responded, not mentioning that she didn't entirely trust the Indian girls nor want to be around them. "But you should definitely consider it. You could learn for all of us. Jan probably wouldn't attend since it is on a Sunday, and he would be against that—and the fact that a woman teaches the class—but it would be good for you. It would be something to do besides empty glasses at Kaska's," she said teasingly.

Josef nodded, embarrassed by her observation, but she was right. He wasted too much time, and money, at Kaska's saloon. He would inquire at the next opportunity, he thought. It would help him in this primarily English-speaking country, and the Indian girls intrigued him too, especially the one with the big smile. Yes, he might have to call on Anna.

The next Sunday after mass when he knocked on Anna's door, a young, blond-haired boy opened it. The boy said politely in German, "Good afternoon! How can I help you?"

"I understand there are English classes held here. I would like to attend them, if possible," Josef replied.

"Yes, my mother does hold lessons. Please come in. My name is Hans," he said as an identical twin came up beside him, "and this is my younger brother, Hector."

Hector punched Hans in the arm, "By two minutes, you *dummkopf*! But I am taller than you and much stronger, too," he boasted.

"You are not!" Hans said, immediately shoving Hector back, beginning to tussle with him.

Mary Barton

Josef smiled at the antics of the young men, as Anna hurried toward them, "Boys, boys, where are your manners? Let the gentleman in. What must he think of us?"

Hector stuck out his tongue at Hans as they moved out of their mother's way.

Anna turned toward Josef and spoke in German, "My apologies, sir. They forget themselves. Please come in. My name is Anna and you are?"

"Josef Riske, madam," he replied, "Jan and Suzanna's cousin from next door. I've been living with them as Jan recovered from his injuries incurred at the mine disaster. Suzanna mentioned that you teach English classes, and if there is room for another student, I would like to learn the language."

"Such a tragedy. May mercies and blessings be upon them. I pray for their poor souls every night. But, yes, of course, we begin at 1:00 o'clock every Sunday afternoon and continue until 4:00 o'clock. I know it is unseemly to teach on Sundays, but it is the only day the men are free to learn. We were just about to begin. The fee is ten cents per lesson."

"Danka," Josef replied, as he fished coins from his pocket and handed them to her.

"Boys, show Mr. Riske to the parlor. I will be there momentarily. Girls," she continued as she hurried over to where the previously seen Indian girls were cleaning coal oil lamps. "To prevent coal oil lamp explosions that can severely injure or kill somebody, we must never turn the wick too low as it continues to burn and creates charcoal, or a crust, which can remain burning. That red heat on the lowered wick can ignite the oil in the lamp. What we must do to prevent that is to first blow out the flame down the lamp chimney, then lower the wick to avoid it expelling smoke. We must keep the wick neatly trimmed clean of the charcoal every day and wash the smoke-blackened glass thoroughly so it can emit more light.

"Good, good, that is the correct way, Little Turtle. There were over 800 fires just last month in New York. We must be careful. Both of you please join us in the parlor when you are finished," she said as she quickly bustled away from them.

There were about eight young men seated around the parlor. They nodded at Josef as he entered and found an empty place to sit. Anna rushed in and made introductions, then handed a sheet of paper with both the German and the corresponding English alphabet neatly printed on it to Josef and said, "Please memorize these before next Sunday. It will help you catch up to where we are.

"Let us begin. As many of you know the best way to learn a new language is to learn the language grammar so you know how to construct sentences; through listening closely to anyone speaking to you in English; and by practicing speaking the language daily."

Picking up a slate with English words printed on it from a table and holding it in front of her, she asked one of the students to read it to her.

"I have to work," he read hesitantly using a thick German accent.

"Very good. And what does this mean in German, Heinrich?" she asked another student. When he responded, 'I has to work', she replied, "Close," with an encouraging smile. Turning the slate over, she showed the same sentence written in German. "You used the correct verb, but the wrong person. Remember that the verb changes according to the subject of the sentence. First person singular is 'I' when you are speaking about yourself. First person plural is 'we' when you are speaking about a group you are in. Second person singular and plural is 'you' when you are speaking about someone else or a group you are talking to. Then the third person singular subject of a sentence is he, she, or it when you are referring to a person or thing. The third person plural subject word to use is 'they' when you are talking about a group or things of which you are not a part. Then the verbs change accordingly. Let's review some more examples."

She proceeded to list the present singular and plural tense forms of the English and German verb "have" — I have, you have, he/she/it has, and we have, you have, and they have. For the verb "do" she listed — I do/don't, you do/don't, he/she/it does/doesn't; we do/don't, you do/don't and they do/don't.

Then she pronounced the present and past tenses singular and plural forms of the verb "be" — I am/was, we are/were; you are/were, you are/were; he/she/it is/was and they are/were.

"If we don't use the correct tense, then people will not be able to easily understand what you are trying to say," she said. Noticing Josef's bewildered look she immediately instructed Green Leaves, the braided-haired Indian girl, to review the correct tenses with the class and asked Little Turtle, 'the sunbeam', to review the pronunciation of the German alphabet with Mr. Riske, so that he could comprehend the differences between the languages.

Startled by the suggestion but pleased with the extra help, Josef nodded, as Little Turtle sat beside him on the chaise lounge. For the rest of the lesson, they practiced the pronunciation of the alphabet until he was certain he knew the correct English pronunciation. During the lesson, he covertly noticed every detail of Little Turtle—her clear-skinned beauty, the strings of beads hanging down to the middle of her chest and her polite demeanor as she sat beside him. When he left for the day, he respectfully thanked her for her help and promised to practice before the next lesson. As he walked home, although suspicious of her heritage and her unknown innate character, he vowed to learn quickly and looked forward to the next lesson.

Introductions

For the rest of the year, Josef religiously attended English classes, gradually improving his English until he could construct sentences with ease. He continued to observe the Indian girls whenever he saw them and found them to be quite well-educated, more than he was for sure. They were generally busy with Anna's children or household tasks, but quiet unless called on to assist the class.

One bright spring afternoon in 1873 after cleaning his militia-provided musket in the backyard and enjoying the sunshine, he heard a crash and yelp of pain from Anna's property. Hurrying over with gun in hand, he entered the carriage shed from where the sounds were emitting. There was Hans, lying on the ground near an overturned wooden barrel, tangled in a fishing net. Josef set down his gun and helped him to his feet, checking for injuries, as Little Turtle rushed toward them.

"It looks like no damage was done," Josef said to Little Turtle. "He might be a little sore after his tumble but I don't think anything is broken."

"You foolish boy!" she exclaimed to Hans. "What were you doing?"

"Hector and I are building a tree fort," he replied rubbing his arm, chagrined at his mishap. "I was trying to reach that hammer," he said pointing to the tool attached to the wall beyond his reach, "so we can build it. I lost my footing while standing on the keg and fell into the fishing net."

"Please try to be more careful or ask for help when you need it. Here," she said, handing him the hammer, "and don't fall out of any trees! Your mother would be very upset." Hans nodded, grabbed the tool and rushed out the door to rejoin Hector.

Josef smiled at Little Turtle, "Those two seem to be quite a handful," he said.

"Yes, they certainly are," she replied. "I sometimes think their energy should be harnessed to more productive activities, but with their father gone to the Great Beyond, Anna allows them more freedom than usual, I think, and indulges them a lot. But that is understandable considering the circumstances."

Josef nodded and said, "Which can or cannot be a good thing. I know from my nephew how quickly children can get into trouble. Of course, they are older than he is and should have more sense." Looking around the shed, he noticed a half barrel with a turtle in it. "What is this?" he asked Little Turtle.

"This is *Tung-ul-ung'-si*, 'smallest turtle' in my language. He is my pet and a reminder of my heritage," she replied with a gentle smile. "I come from the Little Turtle clan of the Lenape, Delaware tribe, which is how I received my name, *We-lung-ung-sil*. After my mother refused to leave her territory to move West with most of my people at the request of the government, she perished during a cholera epidemic and I was sent to live at the Moravian ministry.

"Like the ministry, I care for Tung-ul-ung'-si, as they cared for me. I gather plants, snails and worms, sometimes fish, to feed him. Like turtles, I was 'abandoned' by my mother as they are by theirs, to make my own way. And like them, I, and what remains of my people, have developed a hard outer shell which makes it difficult for enemies to kill or conquer us," she said with a smile, as she nodded at his musket. "Do you hunt?"

"Yes, after work, when I can," Josef nodded and continued, "I'm so sorry for your loss. It must have been difficult for you."

"It was, at first. But like smallest turtle, I rub off my dead 'skin' against the stone of my experiences and grow a new shell as I need it," she said with a confidant smile.

After that encounter, Josef made it a habit of staying after Sunday lessons to talk with Little Turtle and frequently brought her food for Tung-ul-ung'-si. He learned from her that the Moravians were a Protestant congregation that performed the liturgy in the language of the people they were preaching to, an unheard of practice among Catholics, and that they had established a continuous prayer session which had run uninterrupted for 24 hours a day, for 100 years.

They believed strongly in pacificism and the education of everyone, regardless of station in life.

Little Turtle was taught by them that a lifestyle of prayer, worship and a form of communal living was desirable. In this practice personal property was still owned but a simple lifestyle and generosity were considered important. As a result, divisions between social groups and extremes of wealth were eliminated, similar to the ways of her Lenape origins.

Once, while embarrassingly conjugating the word 'love' during a lesson with Little Turtle, she told him of the love-feasts the Moravians practiced. They were services dedicated to emphasizing Christian love where the bonds of kinship were strengthened, as well as to forgive past disputes among themselves. During these feasts, sweetened rolls and tea was served to the accompaniment of music about the benefits of love and harmony from the choir.

According to Little Turtle, the Moravians believed so strongly in unity, regardless of race, ethnicity or class distinction, that even their graveyards, laid out on hilltops called "God's Acre," were organized by gender, age, and marital status rather than family. In their "choir system" cemeteries, every stone was the same size and made of the same material so that no person stood out, even in death. The church motto was: "In essentials, unity; in nonessentials, liberty; and in all things, love."

When he asked her why she had left the Moravians to live with Anna, since she so clearly admired and adhered to the beliefs of her rescuers, she replied that she believed it was a sign from God that it was time to find her own place in the world, as had her matrilineal ancestors. When Anna approached the orphanage for possible help after her husband passed away, she and Green Leaves were interviewed for the positions. "Anna" in the Lenape language meant "mother" and she had been so kind and generous, as her own mother had been, Little Turtle knew she should accept the job. When she later learned that Anna frequently spoke to her deceased husband, she knew she was in the company of a wise woman, and that it was the correct place for her to be.

Although it was a different world than that of her ancestors, to honor her heritage, as well as her new world, she insisted she needed to learn to live with those around her in peace, including the miners. What better place to do that, than with a wise woman who could speak to the spirits?

Although puzzled by some of her beliefs, Josef strengthened his relationship with Little Turtle throughout 1873. They frequently gathered mushrooms and berries with Green Leaves when the weather was nice and he found he could relax, and felt accepted and comfortable around her. She generally had a cheerful disposition, despite the looks their keeping company garnered from the local community. He admired her grace and dignity in those situations, and respected her right to make her own decisions as had her ancestors, regardless of the opinions of others—and was surprised to find himself frequently outraged by those who displayed their disapproval of her and felt indignant on her behalf.

He had to admit, she was a unique, intelligent creature to be admired, not judged because of her heritage. The attraction he was feeling for Little Turtle was both enticing, exciting and disconcerting. He was no longer lonely, and truly admired her playfulness, and the admiring glances toward him that she tried to hide from him. But he wasn't sure what he felt for her was true love or his male nature reacting with rabbit-like breeding inclinations. He knew she made him feel alive, and happy. Something he didn't know if he had ever truly felt, because of the constant war or oppression he had experienced in Poland.

His family probably wouldn't approve of her. To them it would be like him marrying a Russian or a German—someone you could never entirely trust since they had subjugated the Polish people. Unfortunately, much like the Americans were trying to rule the red men: trying to make them into something they weren't or didn't want to be. But once his family got to know Little Turtle, he felt they would like her—if they gave her a chance. The red men were still an unknown factor to him personally. He had heard both sides of their story from the militia and from Little Turtle. The militia saw their dark side; Little Turtle their good. He shook his head. Well, he couldn't solve all of the problems of the world, although he would continue to analyze his feelings and discover what he truly wanted to do.

Jan, in the meantime, realized that his misgivings about Josef's attraction to Suzanna, had been misguided. Suzanna loved his cousin as a dear friend but nothing more. His own insecurities while he was ill compared to Josef's taller, broader, healthier physique had generated fears of betrayal where none existed. Suzanna was, in fact, pregnant once again and content in her household. She was, however, concerned regarding Josef's increasing interest in Little Turtle, but Jan believed that it was a good diversion for Josef in this region of few available women.

Engaging the Enemy

*J*ust after Mayday in 1874, when the Maypole had been merrily wrapped with brightly colored ribbons by singing and dancing maidens, Josef was notified via telegraph to engage in a summer campaign against rogue Lenape warriors who were on the warpath against isolated homesteaders. He had been regularly meeting with the militia for target and drilling practice but had yet to engage an enemy on a battlefield. This campaign was set to eradicate a band of particularly vicious Indians who were on a rampage of destruction, and reportedly, had murdered at least five families of innocent men, women and children.

When he went to inform Little Turtle that he would be leaving, she responded with, "Yes, I know."

"What do you mean, you know? I haven't told anyone but my cousin and boss that I would be leaving," he asked.

"Anna told me. She spoke with the spirits just after the sun hid from us and they said you would be leaving us soon."

"That is nonsense, or great coincidence!" he replied irritably, although he knew Suzanna had been disturbed by the recent eclipse of the sun, too, believing it portended trouble. When she learned of his call to duty, she, too, had been overly concerned at his leaving. She had begged him to reconsider, telling him it wasn't his fight. Why endanger his life? But after all the tales Josef had heard from the older militia members, he believed he was protecting life by going on the campaign, saving those who could not defend themselves, and helping rid the world of murderous vermin.

Jan had been dismayed, as well, but his misgivings had been more about Josef's involvement with taking someone's life. That wasn't something that was easy to live with, especially for someone as self-effacing and gentle as Josef. Josef

The Eagle's Nest

was like an over-sized puppy dog who was friendly but not realizing his own strengths, became remorseful when he accidently hurt someone. Jan himself still recalled horrific memories of the wars in Poland. He believed Josef could defend himself but he didn't want him to suffer from similar harsh events—of watching people torn from their natural state of grace into fragmented bodies and lost souls.

But Josef could not be dissuaded. His honor was at stake to finish what he had started. He was no coward, nor did he want to be branded as one. He knew he couldn't live with himself if he backed away from his duty.

"You know I respect Anna, but her belief that she speaks with ghosts, is a little hard to swallow," Josef responded.

"There are prophets in the Bible—and among my people. God even said his people would prophesize,' she replied. "Joel 2:28 says 'And it shall come to pass afterward, that I will pour out my Spirit on all flesh; your sons and your daughters shall prophesy, your old men shall dream dreams, and your young men shall see visions.'"

"That is prophecy, not speaking to dead people."

"But you believe they live on in the heavenly fields, don't you? If we can hear God, why can we not hear them?" Little Turtle asked fervently. When Josef hesitated to respond to her reasoning, she quickly continued, "But let's not argue on this last day before you leave. Can we walk for a bit?"

"Certainly," he replied, placing her hand on his bent arm. He didn't want to argue either. He was worried about Little Turtle's reaction to what he would be doing with the militia. They immediately headed toward what had become one of their favorite places to visit, a small apple orchard planted by some early settler in a valley surrounded by tall pine trees. Blue dragonflies wove through the brightly colored wildflower embellished ground beneath the labyrinth of trees. Hummingbirds flitted from blossom to blossom drinking their fill of the orchard's life-giving nectar. Sunlight filtered through the gloriously bedecked branches of the trees.

"So you are going to fight," she finally commented, after soaking in the beauty of the day, allowing the scene to mingle with the acceptance she always experienced when she was with Josef.

"I have no choice. Someone is killing innocent people. They must be stopped."

"'Someone' being my people, I assume," she replied with a sigh. "Can you not live in peace?"

"I would love to, but they are not doing so. They are bad people, wantonly killing...." He ceased his explanation and pulled her into his arms. "You know I don't like this, but I can't allow this to continue when I can do something to end it," he said, as he dropped his chin onto the top of her head where her shimmering black hair cascaded like a waterfall to her waist. After resting there for a while feeling the warmth of her body against his, he drew her back, looked into her dark brown eyes, admiring the strength and beauty he saw there, and the next thing he knew, he was raising her chin and lowering his lips to her mouth.

When she didn't resist, and their passion rose with each explorative kiss, they soon found themselves intimately consummating their relationship on a bed of apple blossom petals. It felt right to both of them, regardless of their backgrounds. Words, once so important to them, were unnecessary as they later parted with deep concern on Little Turtle's face, and deep satisfaction and affection on Josef's.

The next day he caught up with the militia in Pittsburgh where Victor greeted him with enthusiasm at the train station. They immediately climbed astride their horses, heading north to the militia's campsite. Although filled with joy at Little Turtle's acceptance of him, he was also nervous and conflicted about what he had promised to do. *Were Jan, Suzanna and Little Turtle right?*

Maybe they wouldn't have to fight, perhaps the Indians would surrender when outnumbered by the militia, and they could just be arrested and put on trial. He hoped it would be so. He knew many of the militiamen had lost friends and family in Indian raids during the encroachment of white people onto their lands, and most of them were not sympathetic to the Indian's plight. On the other side, most Indians were raised to be, and respected in their roles as, warriors. In this new world, they must feel as impotent as the Poles had in Poland, with another nation trying to govern their way of life. They were only doing what they were taught was an admirable trait, striking out to take back their lifestyle, and following the orders of their chiefs. *What was the right thing to do?*

He didn't know if Little Turtle could forgive him if he was forced to kill one of her relatives.

The trail of destruction was easy to follow by the reports of outraged and frightened neighbors who had been spared the violence of the Indians, and the smoldering smoke of recently burned buildings. The troop caught up with the renegades with the help of a converted Lenape guide three days later. The Indian "netap," friend in the Lenape language, discovered the warrior camp beyond a hill and reported their position to the militia just after dawn.

The militia immediately broke camp and followed their flag color-bearer to try to surprise the group before they recovered from their previous night's liquor-imbibed celebration of their latest conquest. Since orders were hard to hear during combat, the commander surveyed the situation and quietly gave instructions to the militia.

Josef was sickened by what he saw in the camp. Scalps of red and blond hair dangled in the morning breeze from lances near the embers of the campfire where twenty reclining Indians lay. His doubt of what was right disappeared at the sight. At the silent motion of his commander, he, along with the troop of 40 soldiers, raced into the valley with muskets primed.

At the sound of pounding horse hooves, the Indians quickly awakened, threw off their blankets, and reached for their weapons. Bare-chested and clothed in only loincloths or buckskin pants, they ran for their ponies and leaped astride their backs. Some reached them in time and some didn't before the militia was upon them.

Josef rode beside Victor as they entered the camp. Gunpowder blasts were followed by thick clouds of smoke from the burnt powder of the heavy muskets yielded by both sides of the skirmish. The noise was deafening and the horses obeyed their riders out of habit, not desire, as their natural inclinations to flee were over-ridden by the dominant humans forcing them to enter the ruckus. Josef's horse was well-trained from hours of practice and rewarded behavior, so much so that it unflinchingly carried Josef directly into the heart of the battle.

Josef watched as Indians fell throughout the area of the ambush by the greater quantity of soldiers, frequently blasted down by more than one bullet strike. Not all of the Indians had guns, so some were shooting arrows at the approaching militiamen. The surprise attack allowed the militia to down most of the Indians still on the ground and race to engage the ones who had made it to their ponies.

Josef was unnerved by the chaos of the fight with bullets and arrows whizzing around him, but aimed his musket at one Indian crouched on the ground who was shooting arrows at any approaching soldier. Before he could get his shot off, the wolf-tattooed Indian sighted on Victor riding beside him, aimed true and shot an arrow through his heart.

"God have mercy," Josef said, as he killed the Indian then raced to where Victor had fallen from his horse.

Saying Goodbye

It's all my fault, Josef thought, blaming himself. *If I had only gotten that shot off earlier, Victor would still be alive. God forgive me.* Anguished that he could have prevented his friend's death, he didn't know if he could ever forgive himself.

He sent a telegram to Jan and Suzanna informing them of what had happened and returned Victor's body to his sister. Grief-stricken, she decided that Victor should be buried at Gettysburg beside her brother-in-law. Josef accompanied her there where her sorrow, his remorse, the military taps, and the 21-gun salute performed by the militia nearly broke his heart.

After Victor's funeral, he visited his cousin Auguste's grave and wept openly. Here was the result of man's inhumanity to man. Lives had been taken that should never have been taken. The ugliness and finality of death chilled him to the bone. He didn't know if he could ever yield a gun again. He didn't know if he could ever look at another Indian with anything other than bitterness. He didn't know how he could survive his sorrow and guilt.

When a fellow soldier invited him to meet at a local tavern to drink to the deceased's honor, Josef shook off his remorse and joined his comrades. A drink was just what he needed. Josef had to admit, he *was* deeply gratified that he had been able to pay his respects to his cousin Auguste, although he would rather it had been under different circumstances.

"You should be proud of him," his companion commented, as they drank to the memory of Victor. "He fought bravely with great courage, and we ended up getting every one of those heathens. They won't be terrifying decent people again!"

Josef nodded. He was proud of Victor. He had fearlessly given his life to protect the living and his death, although unwelcome, encouraged Josef to reach his own goals despite any obstacle that stood in his way. Having barely escaped death himself, Josef *would* ensure that Victor's sacrifice would not go unrewarded. He vowed he would live as good a life as he could, hopefully without the necessity of taking more life.

When Jan and Suzanna received the news they were both dismayed about Victor's demise. Suzanna was particularly heart-broken and frightened by the violence of it all: it made her mistrust the savages even more. Victor had been too good a man to have met his death at such a young age. It was beyond comprehension. She could only weep in anguish at the Devil's deed.

When Little Turtle heard the results of the raid, her protective shell hardened even further. She had never met Victor but she did know the Lenape warriors who had been killed by the militia. Several of them had been orphans like she and Green Leaves, but they had not embraced the Morovian upbringing they had received.

The band of Indians blamed the white men for the demise of their parents and their lifestyle. As soon as they could manage it, the rebels had left the benevolent school to live on their own and reclaim their heritage. Hunger, alcohol, and revenge had driven them to attack the white settlers. Although it broke her heart, Little Turtle couldn't forgive Josef for his part in their demise and rebuffed his attempts to speak to her again. She just couldn't accept that he had been a willing participant in the raid and hadn't chosen an avenue other than violence.

Josef was conflicted and chagrined by Little Turtle's refusal to see him. After numerous attempts to contact her, he finally resigned himself to the fact that their relationship was over, and visited Kaska's saloon on a more frequent basis.

The only bright aspect of that year was when Suzanna gave birth to their daughter, Mary. After there was another mine explosion that blew huge pieces of timber up into the air, some falling on, and crashing through, the roofs of nearby houses, Jan and Josef decided that it was time to move on. Having completed their contracts, and saved enough money to move west, in the spring of 1875 they would travel to their uncle's home in Winona and from there to Dakota Territory for they knew: "he whose coach is drawn by hope has poverty for a coachman." That would not be them. Like males of all species, they would claim and defend their property.

The Great Comet of 1874, visible to the naked eye in June and July in the northern hemisphere, awed the educated, scared the ignorant, and was fodder for many church sermons. The sight of the comet for such an extended period of time, was followed by the news that government troops were being sent to Dakota Territory. Like the comet trail, the troops had a contingency of followers including 115 red river carts filled with supplies, 100 head of cattle, several forges, and mowing machines to feed the livestock. They reported that in August they encountered a band of 30 Sioux.

The group was composed primarily of hungry women and children. They put up a tent, smoked a peace pipe with the soldiers, and accepted gifts from them. The lonely soldiers received "gifts" from the Sioux as well—fleas and lice—and combated those fierce critters by rubbing their bodies with oil of juniper. They then deloused their clothes by setting them on ant hills and letting the industrious ants gorge on the bugs.

The newspapers reported that the Canadians were also attempting to handle the Indian population better—by governing the whiskey traders who were creating havoc amongst the Indians. The whiskey trade induced many Indians to stop hunting leaving them with no goods with which to trade. That frequently resulted in drunken fights outside the walls of the forts between the Indians who could buy whiskey and those who couldn't.

Other unethical traders concocted fake 'whiskey' composed of water, chewing tobacco, tea, ginger and blackstrap syrup to make it taste like rum, and then sold it to the Indians. Some Indians died after drinking it from shock or poisoning.

The Northwest Canadian mounted police were sent to Winnipeg, just north of Dakota Territory, when the traders started taking further advantage of the Indians by giving them canned good labels instead of real money for their expensive furs.

After three years of service at $.75 per day, the mounted police were rewarded with 160 acres of free land. After reading the reports Jan was encouraged to investigate the area south of there even more—the territory was becoming civilized, safer, and there was plenty of land still available.

Reuniting

The Riske's journey west began by taking the train to Erie and waiting two weeks in an inexpensive hotel with their toddlers before the *St. Louis* steamship had enough passengers and goods to traverse the Great Lakes to reach Minnesota. The wait frustrated Jan, as he was forced to spend some of his much hoarded funds for food and the hotel—and he wanted to be on his way! He had already been delayed five years by fate and was more than ready to reunite with his family and reach his new home.

Suzanna was still nursing Mary but August was drinking from a cup like an adult, and demonstrated his ability by carrying his tin cup around and scooping up any water he found, grinning widely when he came across easily accessible potage. In the fervor of finally being on their way, none of the adults noticed when August wandered a short distance from them and drank from a stagnant pool of water mixed with human refuse along the dock.

Lake Erie was clear of ice en route to Detroit, as was Lake Michigan when they traveled to Chicago and Milwaukee. Suzanna became only mildly concerned when August started vomiting shortly after beginning the boat trip. She assumed it was a case of seasickness caused by the swaying steamship. They had to wait a day on Lake Superior due to still-frozen waters but reached Duluth, Minnesota safely. They rushed to catch the next train to St. Paul where they made arrangements to board a paddleboat to Winona. Before they boarded the boat, they sent a telegram to Martin of their expected arrival time. By then August had developed a severe case of watery diarrhea. Suzanna cleaned him up and fed him some dry bread and tea, hoping the boat wouldn't induce further illness during the 30-mile trip downriver. *What an inconvenient time for him to fall ill!*

When they disembarked, Uncle Martin hurried up to Jan and Josef overcome with emotion and hugged them fiercely saying, "Finally we meet again! What has it been, at least 15 years? I'm so sorry neither I nor Julius could make it to Castle Garden, but things were rather difficult then," he said with a melancholy look, remembering the death of his grandson and his daughter-in-law's long recovery. "But blessed be Jesus Christus for your safe journey!"

"Please do not apologize. We managed and understood completely. No one could have expected you to make a journey at such a time. Please allow me to express my sincere condolences for your loss," Jan said

"Likewise," Uncle Martin replied, "it seems we have much in common. I miss my brother Piotor and my son Auguste to this day, God rest their souls. It broke my heart to hear of your friend's return to God, although I am sincerely grateful that you were able to visit Auguste's grave," he said to Josef. "They did what needed to be done. Now they both truly can rest in peace."

"Yes, we miss them all greatly, but they are in God's hands now," Josef replied, acknowledging his uncle's gratitude and their shared sorrows.

"Uncle Martin, let me introduce you to my family. This is my wife Suzanna, our son August, and daughter Mary," Jan said proudly.

Martin smiled broadly at his deceased son's namesake, and heartily embraced them all, welcoming and admiring them each in turn. "Blessed be. Let's get your things on the wagon, so we can get you settled and celebrate properly."

Motioning two strong young men standing beside a wagon toward them, he said, "You remember your cousins Julius and Frank, don't you?"

Jan grinned broadly, hardly recognizing the men from the boys they had been since they last saw each other. He heartily shook each of their hands in turn, saying. "Finally we meet again! It is so good to see you! It's been too long a time."

"Yes, it has!" they responded sincerely, and stepped to Josef to shake his hand. Then nodding to Jan's family, "Let's get you loaded." They quickly placed everything into the wagon, made sure Suzanna and the children were comfortably seated, and were soon on their way.

"What news of Dakota Territory?" Jan eagerly inquired.

"Good news," Julius replied, smiling broadly. "I've been following the reports and learned there is an area called *Les Grandes Fourches*, Grand Forks, which is where the Red River and the Red Lake River meet which the French traders apparently used as a trading location with the Indians. A Captain Griggs and his crew were stranded there when his steamboat unexpectedly froze in the river during an early cold snap in 1870, forcing them to spend the winter there. They evidently have established a settlement and U.S. post office, and have begun platting the community. That area is fairly unsettled, so it seems a likely place to check out with water nearby for fishing and irrigation."

"And the land is still free?" Josef asked.

"Well, practically," Julius responded. "There is a small fee to register the claim, other than that we just need the wherewithal to farm and create shelter. We can thank the Yankees for that! They wanted individual farmers to own farms to prevent the southern slave-owners from grabbing up all of the land and using slaves to harvest large tracts of property."

Frank joined in the conversation adding, "In 1862 President Lincoln signed the *Homestead Act* so that any adult who had never taken up arms against the government—now including freed slaves and women—could file an application to claim a federal land grant. Then in 1873 the *Timber Culture Act* was passed for an initial allotment of 160 acres that requires pioneers to plant 40 acres of trees over several years, but has no residency requirement. So we can do both! We can get a whole quarter-section, 320 acres, for 18 dollars for each claim, or temporarily place a claim for $10. I'm telling you, America truly is a heaven on earth!

"All we need to do is find our land, stake it, and settle on it for at least 6 months out of a year. That will work perfectly as we can go there in the spring, plant, harvest, build our homes, and move our families there once that is accomplished. We can work here through the winter until we're ready to move completely to the property."

"Are you planning to move there, too?" Jan asked Martin.

"I probably won't," Martin admitted. "I'm getting too old to do that kind of work again, and I have my farm here that I am happy with, but it is a great opportunity for you young men to take advantage of. Free land is well worth the effort to get it."

Nodding at his comment, noticing how aged his uncle had become, Jan asked, "I'm sorry you won't be joining us. But maybe you will change your mind later once we get settled. What kind of work is available around here?"

"There are a lot of jobs working on the railroad and steamboat lines, as well as wheat milling, and lumber sawmills," Martin responded. "Over 1,000 steamboats stop here as its one of the largest shipping ports on the Mississippi River. It started out as a Dakota Sioux village called *Keoxa* but became *Winona* after a local chief named it from the Dakota Indian word 'We-no-nah,' which means first-born daughter.

"And we have quite a Polish community now after the first Kashubian family, the Bronks, moved here in 1855," he continued. "The word spread and many more have followed them here even since you emigrated. That's Sugar Loaf, the hill just beyond the bluffs," he said pointing in that direction. "We live just south of there. But like you, the opportunity to own free land is something that only a fool would not take advantage of, and our family has never been known to be fools. We'll make plans in good time later but now we raise our glasses to your safe arrival!" he said affectionately clapping Jan on his back again.

Divine Intervention

Suzanna was not feeling well herself when they landed as morning sickness once again accompanied her newest pregnancy. With August experiencing diarrhea, they were not the best houseguests as they met the rest of the family. Despite their infirmities they were enthusiastically invited to board with their relatives until they could find jobs, housing, and add more money to their coffers for their land claims. Martin's second wife would watch the little ones while they searched for work. Jan quickly found a job at a local lumber mill as did Suzanna at a nearby wheat processing plant. Josef was elated to find work at the local stable when they learned of his experience with horses.

It was a joy becoming reacquainted with their relatives, and they immediately felt at home, reminiscing about occasions in their past and telling of what had occurred since they had last been together. But fate continued to interfere in their lives. August was not improving. He was lethargic, experiencing muscle cramps, and losing weight. They were using as many home remedies as they could think of to help him but his eyes were sunken in, his skin was cold, and his feet and hands were becoming wrinkly. When Suzanna returned home from her second day of work, his skin looked bluish-gray, so they rushed him to a doctor who pronounced August had the "blue death," cholera, and passed away several hours later.

Suzanna wrapped him in her arms, cried in anguish, and could not be consoled. *How could this happen?* She still had Mary and another baby on the way but she couldn't understand the purpose of it all. *What had she done that had caused death to take her beloved son at only four years old?* She knew it was common for children to pass away in this world of uncertainties, and Julius's wife who had lost her own son completely empathized with her, but Suzanna couldn't help but blame this country. Not only had it injured her family but it had caused her to lose much that she held dear. When she was finally persuaded to release her beloved son's body, she despaired and despised everything she looked at.

Lamenting profusely himself, Jan tried to comfort Suzanna. He wrapped her in his arms but she could not respond with anything but coldness. They buried August three days later near Julius's son's grave on May 18th and notified their family in Poland of their misfortune. As the disease was not contagious but the result of polluted water, it was not required to isolate the rest of the family, although they did boil all of their clothes and scrubbed everything clean that August may have touched.

In her grief over the next month, Suzanna repeatedly tried to convince Jan to leave this accursed country but he responded by deciding to travel to Dakota Territory as soon as possible. Suzanna was infuriated by his decision but could not dissuade him. Agreeing with Proverbs 21:19 that stated: "It is better to live in a desert land than with a quarrelsome and fretful woman," Jan decided to allow time to heal his wife. He didn't have the temperament to indulge in self-pity but accepted what was, although he felt the loss of August as fiercely as did Suzanna. Even though Jan believed without doubt that God decreed who would live or die, that didn't help his feelings of intense remorse for his sin of not protecting his family. He reasoned that despite the fact that Suzanna missed Poland and her relatives, and was devastated by the death of their son, war was still raging in Europe and life would be no better there than here.

After Martin chanced upon one of their arguments, he later gently reminded Jan of the Polish proverb: "no fish without bones; no woman without a temper," and Jan agreed with him. He loved Suzanna with all of his heart and soul. She had been nothing but the best, most desirable wife, mother and helpmate for which a man could hope but he also wouldn't give up all he had worked for before he had even seen it.

Josef discovered he was conflicted about joining his cousins on the journey west. He was surprised to find he was both unable, and unwilling, to leave a job he discovered he truly loved. Strange as it seemed, the tangy smell of horses, leather and hay had brought him back to life, and given him a sense of peace that he didn't realize he had lost.

While pondering the decision to go west to Dakota Territory, he realized he had died after the fight with the Lenape as surely as had Victor. Being around the horses had awoken him from a depression that had been caused by his part in Victor's death, the memory of killing another human being, and the pain of Little Turtle's rejection of him. When a herd of wild horses from the frontier were delivered to the stable just before they were to leave, and his boss needed his expertise to help train them, excited by the opportunity, Josef decided he would let his cousins scout the territory while he wrangled with the unbroken horses. He could join them later once they scouted out the situation.

At the end of June, Julius, Frank and Jan would travel upriver to catch the 30-mile per hour train in St. Paul to reach the end of the railroad line at Fisher's Landing in Dakota Territory. Suzanna would barely speak to Jan when he left, although she did cling to him, terrified that she might never see him again. She resigned herself to the circumstances but could not yet forgive his decision nor his abandonment of her.

❈

Jan, Julius and Frank all became better acquainted, learning each other's personalities and quirks on their way. Frank was a bachelor and the youngest at 27-years-old, Jan was 28, while Julius was the oldest at 30. Frank was eager for adventure while Julius, like Jan, was ambitious and ready to find a permanent home for his family.

On their journey Julius and Frank both spoke English well and questioned those they met for news of Grand Forks. Everyone they spoke with was friendly and eager to offer advice. One man warned them to watch out for snakes along the river, as a snake killing competition had just been held the previous month and over 1,000 reptiles had been killed. Another told them not to eat any meat from dead buffalo they might come across as a group called "White Wolfers" poisoned buffalo carcasses so that wolves and other animals would feed on them and die. The Wolfers then took the pelts and sold them for $2.50 to $3.00 each.

After crossing almost the full width of Minnesota by train, with their horses in a boxcar, at Fisher's Landing 15 miles east of Grand Forks, they disembarked, gathered their horses and took the Fisher Trail on horseback north towards Grand Forks. They could have taken a steamboat to Grand Forks but had decided to bring their own horses—one borrowed from Uncle Martin for Jan—to follow the trail to get a better feel for the country.

Unaccustomed to riding a horse on a regular basis, after several miles Jan felt every movement of his horse run painfully through his widespread thighs and torso. The view, however, kept him distracted from his discomfort. Flocks of hundreds of geese disturbed by their passage lifted from the flat, grass-covered plains where their nests were hidden, and honked in protest that the group had invaded their territory. Crops of white clouds swayed in the brilliant blue sky.

Jan smiled with wonder as flickertail ground squirrels stopped their manic chores and watched them briefly, waving their tails in consternation, before hurrying back to their destinations. They all exclaimed in excitement as they witnessed a huge herd of deer grazing in the endless land. Near the Red River garter snakes spooked the horses, causing each of them to rein in their mounts for better control. They passed patches of wild chokecherries swaying in the breeze while armies of bees feasted on the wild flowers blossoming throughout the open country.

En route they were surprised to encounter a 500 Red River cart train from Pembina, a city near the Canadian border, on its way to St. Paul. They watched in astonishment as 700 white, Indian and mixed-breeds guided ox-drawn carts loaded with beaver, wolf, raccoon, fox, mink, bear, and buffalo pelts slowly meandered past them.

Somewhat awed by the wealth carried on those carts, and excited that such riches could be theirs, the Riskes learned from one of the trail guides that the six- to seven-foot diameter, two-wheeled Red River carts were originally designed by the Metis for crossing streams and snow-melted swamps along their moisture-laden way. The carts never overturned because of their width and could haul up to 800 pounds of goods. The wheels themselves were covered with buffalo hides that were put on wet then dried to shrink in place, creating a tire that rarely fell off, and were built light enough to traverse the muddy plains. The cousins were thoroughly impressed by the ingenious invention of the

The Eagle's Nest

supposedly ignorant Indians. They learned that the troupe's month long, one-way trip, would be rewarded with supplies of hardware, dry goods, tobacco, and alcohol to take back to their homes.

Grateful for the unexpected company that allowed them to let down their guard on the trail, they soon arrived at the Red River landing site. There they led their horses onto a flat, rail-sided ferryboat with loading ramps on each end for the journey across the water to Grand Forks. As they traversed the short expanse, they saw a Red River Transportation Line steamboat filled with steel rails on its way north for the Canadian Pacific Railroad Company. Once on land they were impressed to see a boat building and repair yard, and a stagecoach office near the dirt landing port.

As they rode up the streets that were deeply rutted from recent rains, they came across a sawmill, grist mill, and the dirt- and bark-covered post office cabin. Further along the path there were several wood framed houses, a couple of saloons and general stores, and at least one boarding house. Mrs. Woolley's Millinery Store, the Hudson Bay Company store and the North Western Hotel dominated the small business district. They headed for the North Western Hotel for a decent night's sleep, a good meal, a bath, clean clothes, and picked up *The Plaindealer* newspaper to learn of the local news.

Wonders Abound

The next morning after breakfast they headed to a local saloon and the post office to ask the "old-timers" about the Indian situation, the available land, and the rules governing staking claims. They were pleasantly surprised on all accounts.

The resident *Chippewa* Indians, also known as the *Ojibwa*, were a peaceful tribe and enemies of the warring Sioux, whom they had primarily forced out of their area pushing them further to the west. The Chippewa were farmers who also fished and hunted game to supplement their women's cultivation of crops and harvesting of wild rice. The rice, they learned, grew in the shallow water of small lakes and slow-flowing streams.

The Chippewa frequently visited the forts and Grand Forks to trade their maple syrup, corn, pemmican, rice, buckskins, moccasins, and canoes. They were a congenial lot and had shown the pioneers how to fish through holes in the ice, and used snow sleds filled with supplies pulled by their trained dogs to traverse about 70 miles per day in the winter. They even created tiny leather boots for the animals' feet so they weren't injured where the ice was jagged.

More importantly the Riskes were delighted to learn that about 35 miles to the north and slightly west of the Red River there was a lake, with fresh water streams that fed into it from the Forrest River, which had land near it yet to be claimed. This lake area also held some elm, willow and cottonwood groves on it. They were told that the Red River did hold sturgeon in the winter, but because of its northern flow, would periodically flood in the springtime when the river melt would back up into its still-frozen Canadian reaches. The lake region would be a better place to stake claims as it was too far from the Red

River to be flooded by the backup of water that couldn't make it through its ice-jammed Canadian section.

While at the saloon, a friendly half-breed inquired if they wanted a guide to that area, as he knew it well. After learning from the bartender he was competent and could be trusted, they negotiated a price for his services, and made plans to meet in the morning. They thanked their informants, went to a general store to gather supplies for their journey, and the next morning they packed their gear and set out north into the maiden land with their guide, Flying Goose. As they traveled along the crooked Red River, the sky was clear and bright, and seemed to hold the glitter of treasures to come.

As they rode they encountered several homesteads but primarily flat virgin land filled with brush, prairie grass, and cottonwood trees along the river banks. As the day heated up attacks by swarms of mosquitoes made them disgruntled. While they rode, although the constant light Dakota wind helped, they zigzagged their horses to create an even stronger breeze to dissuade the bloodsuckers. When they decided to stop for lunch, they established a smoke pot to help keep the mosquitoes at bay while they ate.

When Flying Goose offered them some pemmican that he pulled from a rawhide bag, and they looked at it with suspicion, he explained, "It is a mixture of dried buffalo meat ground into powder, combined with fat and dried powdered chokecherries. It can be eaten raw, in a stew, or fried with vegetables. We take it with us on long journeys since it is lightweight and nutritious when game is hard to find."

The Riskes were polite and each tried some, commenting that it wasn't bad. Curious, Julius asked Flying Goose, "We haven't come across any buffalo yet. Are there many in this area?"

"Some still wander this territory but most of the big herds are about a week's ride west of here. My people generally go to those areas in the spring and autumn to hunt for their yearly supplies."

"Have you been on any of those hunts?" Frank asked.

"Yes, a few. The rules are fairly strict."

"What do you mean?"

"It takes a lot of men and women to engage in a hunt. The last one I was on," Flying Goose explained, "we took 1,200 tongues, which means many hunters and helpers must stalk, kill and process the buffalo.

"Leaders are selected to make sure everyone stays together and follows the directions of the scouts and elders. No one is allowed to hunt until permission is given, and that can be difficult in the spring when food supplies are low. If anyone disobeys, it can ruin a hunt, so they are punished by having their belongings cut up, or can even be flogged for any kind of disobedience. It sounds harsh, but buffalo hunts are the most important way we have of feeding ourselves, so orders must be followed, or we could be starving the families that depend on our success," Flying Goose replied.

"How do you go about hunting a herd of buffalo?" Julius asked.

Flying Goose thought a moment then responded, "The females are the preferred game as they have the most tender meat and pliable hides. They usually run at the front of the herd since they are smaller and faster than the older bulls. But the bulls are wary and when they sense our presence within about 500 paces, they paw the ground or curve their tails, and signal the herd to run. The best way to kill them is to hit them in the heart with a bullet or an arrow placed just behind and beneath their left shoulders."

"How do you proceed when faced with hundreds of head in a herd?"

"We surround and stalk them so they will run in a desired direction. We start slowly then gradually increase our speed until we reach the highest speed possible. Each man carries extra arrows in his shoulder bag, or if he is fortunate to own a gun, he carries spare musket balls in his mouth. After firing his weapon, he shakes gunpowder into the muzzle, and spits a ball down the barrel of the gun, then fires it again. It can be extremely dangerous hunting. The hunters have to be careful as their horses can trip on rough ground or gopher holes, breaking their legs and flinging their riders into the path of the stampeding herd. The huge beasts then send trampled riders on to their Maker.

"But that is the way of life. Once downed, we skin the buffalo, dry the meat, and preserve the pelts. The Great Spirit provides for our people as He has for many generations."

Amazed by the revelations of their obviously well-organized hunts, the cousins quickly broke camp and made it to the lake by early afternoon. The Riskes were excited by what they saw. They traversed the length of the Forrest River and set their sights on a flat area perfect for farming several miles from the lake. They found the river banks were steep and pliable enough in one area, with trees nearby, to construct a dugout to live in while they began cultivating their crops. They chose property close to each other on either side of the river so all would benefit from the clearest water and most flat, fertile black earth they had ever seen.

They camped that night and the next morning Flying Goose and Jan were awakened by the call of an eagle lifting from its nest, circling their property, then heading toward the lake to harvest the abundant God-provided bounty. Flying Goose smiled broadly at the sound, grabbed his pouch of sacred tobacco, and released a prayer of gratitude to the Creator. At the same time Jan made the sign of the cross silently thanking God for leading them to this promised land. Both men noticed the other's reverence and acknowledged it with a nod. Both unknowingly believed that God had just informed them that they were in the right place, at the right time, and were just where they should be.

That day they staked the land, camped there another night, then returned to Grand Forks to file their claims. They gathered the supplies they would need to create their living quarters, and begin clearing and broadcasting seed on the land. Three happier men could not be found anywhere in the region.

The Hand of God

On their return the next day, the Riske cousins again were guided by Flying Goose, this time being more observant of the route they were taking. Flying Goose pointed out several landmarks by which to navigate, and wigwams to the south of the lake where some of his people still lived. Although most of the Chippewa had moved to a nearby reservation, there were a number of domed lodges in addition to others with pointed tops made of birch or juniper bark, and willow saplings. Near the river he showed them dabbling ducks, who feed primarily off the surface of the water, inspecting the flowering heads of wild rice on top of the stream.

"How is the rice harvested?" Julius asked.

"We row to a stand of rice and bend the plants over the boat and use wooden knockers to gently brush the mature grain into the canoe. The *manoomin*, wild rice, is then stored in woven cedar pouches," he explained. "The 'puddle' ducks you see rarely dive, as their feet are smaller than diving ducks, but they are strong fliers, and walk well on land. Puddle ducks jump straight up from the water to fly, while diving ducks run across the water to gain momentum."

After Jan's initial reservations of taking advice from an Indian were dispelled when he led them to their ideal land claims, he smiled broadly every time Frank or Julius would interpret whatever Flying Goose said. While Jan understood some of what Flying Goose would say, he wasn't fluent enough to comprehend all of what he said. He did however have to admire the knowledge, character, and stamina of the man. Flying Goose had been nothing but helpful and friendly to the Polish cousins.

He had been the one to point out the ideal spot for them to claim their land. He had been the one to indicate what would be needed to shelter themselves from inclement weather and store their goods, but not be too difficult to build. He had been the first one to put pickaxe to dirt to start the soddy, and was the first one up at dawn felling nearby trees for the dugout entrance and support beams when they were needed. Once all of that had been accomplished, he had been the one to offer to help them cultivate their ground.

He would frequently gather eggs from nearby nests for breakfast and never came back from the river without a string of fish he had caught. He showed them where berries could be picked, where maple trees could be tapped, and pointed out animal trails to place traps to the best advantage.

After a few weeks of hard labor, one evening while relaxing before sleep, the cousins asked Flying Goose how he came to learn English so well. He replied that during a particularly hard winter his grandfather had traded his mother to an English soldier at one of the forts for a gun, a bottle of alcohol and a few blankets. He was the result of their union and had learned both languages while living at the fort for almost ten years. When his father became lonely for his own people and more civilization, he retired from the military and returned east, abandoning Flying Goose's mother, who returned with her son to her tribe.

"That must have been difficult for you," Julius commented.

"It was at first. I missed my father, but I quickly learned the Indian way of life in which you alternately feast or starve. We initially survived with the few items my dad had left us and by trading 10 beaver skins for a gun and ammunition, and another two pelts for a couple of steel traps. I learned to hunt and trap better, and traded my furs for several knives, an axe, and some food.

"My mother cooked and processed my catches, tanned the leather and fashioned them into clothing and moccasins. She dressed the game for me, and made willow frames to stretch and cure the raw pelts over. We built our own lodge, gathered firewood, wild berries and roots. She showed me how to construct a canoe by stripping birch trees of their bark, and stitching and gluing the pieces to the canoe skeleton, then lined it with melted pine pitch or spruce gum to prevent leaks. We then harvested the wild rice along with the geese and ducks," he said with a smile. "In the winter we wove leather strips into a supporting willow web to use as snowshoes to reach my trap line. We survived."

He shrugged, "Since I knew English, I was able to trade my abilities for whatever else we needed. It has worked out well enough."

The Riskes were managing to clear and cultivate about one-quarter acre a day with the help of their horses, a couple of scythes and a plow. It was hard labor in the hot, humid temperatures but they developed a steady, balanced, rhythm to make it through each day. By the end of July, they had planted as much as would grow in time for harvest, with their muskets always within arm's length. No other Indians bothered them, although they would see them occasionally observing them at a distance. At those times, Flying Goose would leave for the evening but be back at dawn. After one such meeting, Flying Goose asked Julius to interpret something he wanted to speak to Jan about. Curious, Julius immediately agreed.

"Some of my people are concerned. Evidently one of our ancient burial grounds resides on the property you just claimed. I was unaware of this but since I was working with you, they asked me to approach you about honoring their ancestors and not disturbing their resting places."

Jan was shocked when Julius told him what Flying Goose had just said. *He had an Indian burial ground on his property? The devil take you*, he thought.

"I can show you where it is. It is not a large area, but their relatives are hoping you will not disturb the graves."

Jan responded immediately, "Of course I would not disturb those taken by God. Can you show me tomorrow where this area is, so that I won't accidentally disturb it?"

Flying Goose smiled in relief and said, "We can leave after breakfast. It's not far."

Frank chose to stay and clear more ground. As the rest of them rode to the site, Jan asked Julius to ask Flying Goose about the Chippewa spiritual beliefs. Flying Goose complied by explaining that they believed that everything alive is spiritual and nothing is held in higher regard than anything else. Because of that they thank the plants and animals they consume for giving their lives for the Indians' sustenance. According to *Gitchie Manitou*, the "Supreme Being," the Chippewa were just another element of nature, so their main goal as a people was to live in harmony with nature and respect all dwellers on the earth.

Jan heartily agreed with Flying Goose and the Chippewa belief system as it was very similar to his Christian beliefs. Although he believed man was given dominion over nature, he too was aware that the taking of any life was a gift for which to be grateful. He did agree that man needed to learn to live together in peace. War had killed too many innocent people. That Devil's work needed to be stopped.

In the Chippewa belief system, each animal had spiritual importance. The eagle was believed to be the Great Spirit's "prayer carrier" and messenger. When they prayed, the Chippewa would envision themselves turning into eagles so that their prayers would reach, and be answered by, the Creator.

Jan smiled in astonishment at that comment, remembering his own eagle message to move to America. *The workings of the Lord are unending*, he thought.

To the Chippewa the bear claw symbolized healing, the eagle feather strength, and tobacco honesty. Smoking a peace pipe of tobacco was considered the most respectful way of interacting with others and asking for what you needed.

As they approached the burial grounds, the Riskes could see that the Chippewa did not bury their dead in the ground but erected a "spirit-house" of stone or timber over the body. The fifteen graves they saw each held a wooden marker with the deceased's clan sign on it. Some were decorated with animal claws, feathers, strings of shell, or porcupine weavings attached to posts beside the graves, most of which were bedraggled and worn from the elements.

Jan bowed his head and prayed for their souls, and told Flying Goose again that their remains would be safe on his property, although he did request that no more be buried there. Flying Goose readily agreed. He said this family group had all perished of the white man's disease, smallpox, many years back, but their relatives would be grateful for his promise.

When the wheat ripened, the Riskes cut their crops with scythes, separated the grain from the stalks with flails, and sacked it to haul to Grand Forks when the weather became cold and they left for the winter. They sold their wheat in town, left their tools with Flying Goose, who had agreed to keep an eye on their claims until they returned in the spring. After reaching Fisher's Landing they returned the same way they had come to Winona.

Treasures Found

Their homecoming was a welcome one. Everyone was eager to hear the news of what had happened. Suzanna met Jan with a huge smile almost as wide as her belly. She was so relieved to see him returned to her in one piece, she immediately forgave his absence. She had prayed for his safety daily and was glad that God had answered her prayers, although she was shocked at their accommodations. *They were living in a cave?*

Jan insisted it was well-built and secure, and did not go far into the land, so there shouldn't be any cave-ins. It was merely a place to keep them out of inclement weather and protect their tools. He assured her he would have a cabin built for the family before he brought them to live there.

After hearing of the fertile land, the abundant game and wildlife, and the fresh, readily available water, the women were satisfied that their husbands had chosen well, and with diligence they could create a new life for themselves. The men returned to work and began making plans for what they would need to build houses for their families on their property, and to purchase the materials they would need to plant and harvest their crops.

Suzanna was uncomfortable with the news of their friendship with Flying Goose: she didn't know if she could ever trust any Indian after the death of Victor. She was equally appalled by the fact that there was a graveyard on their property! But the wonders of the land Jan described eased her misgivings. She had never seen him so enthusiastic about anything, other than her and their children. His excitement about their property was contagious, and the reality of owning their own home outright made her heart sing with happiness. They would be the lords and ladies of a great deal of land, and their children could prosper away from cities that were filled with disease. Never did she want to lose another child of hers: she knew she couldn't bear it. At the revelations of the riches awaiting them, she decided to place her faith in Jan—for now.

While he was securing their future she had become good friends with Julius's wife, Amelia, and they had been busy taking care of the children, preparing for their growing families, and sewing quilts that they would need in the cold country to which they would be moving.

Amelia and Eva had introduced Suzanna to the Polish community in Winona while the men were away, making Suzanna almost feel at home being able to speak her native language with other women. It had relieved the grief, isolation, and loneliness she had been feeling, and gave her the intimacy and commiseration that only women could provide to one another.

Josef had regained his confidence while he settled into his job and impressed his boss, Vincent, with his expertise throughout the summer. He found he arose eagerly each morning and was giddy with happiness every time he entered a corral. One bright summer day when a new shipment of horses had been delivered, Josef immediately began lassoing and beginning the breaking process. Working steadily throughout the morning, only when he stopped for lunch did Josef realize that he had an audience.

As he removed his hat and knocked the dust off it by hitting it against his thigh, his boss motioned him over to where he stood with a striking young woman. Hair the color of autumn leaves fell to the waist of the young woman's pink and white gingham dress. Her blue eyes twinkled with pleasure as Josef approached.

"I'd like you to meet my daughter, Frances," Vincent said to Josef. "Frances, this is Mr. Riske."

"It's a pleasure to meet you, Mr. Riske! My father has told me so much about you, but now I can see for myself how talented you are!" she said with a smile.

Josef, blushing deep red at the compliment, replied, "How kind of both of you. Please call me Josef."

"Frances has been around horseflesh since she was a baby. I have had a difficult time reminding her that she is a woman now, and had to ban her from breaking more horses herself. I could barely get her to leave her buckskins behind!" Vincent remarked with obvious pride. "She brought us a sampling of her cooking today, though. Why don't we settle over here and enjoy the picnic lunch she brought?"

Frances smiled in chagrin at her father's revelations, while glancing at Josef, who replied, "Thank you! I'd love to."

They walked over to a grove of trees and placed a tablecloth on the ground where Frances began removing fried chicken, biscuits and a fresh rhubarb pie from her basket.

"I hope you like chicken, Josef."

Josef nodded, having a hard time ignoring his reaction to Frances. The woman was a goddess! Her sun-bronzed skin accentuated the firm muscles of someone who was not afraid of indoors or outdoors work, while her cool summer dress clung to her provocative figure. *How had the burly Vincent fathered such a vision?* Josef wondered.

After Vincent was abruptly called away to attend to a potential customer, Frances and Josef enjoyed the picnic lunch as they got to know each other. Josef rapidly downed the chicken after the first bite, taking second and third helpings to savor the delicious treat. Pleased to find that he enjoyed her cooking, Frances relaxed and enthusiastically shared her opinions as she and Josef discussed the merits of the new herd. Josef discovered she was not only an excellent cook but a good judge of horseflesh as well.

All summer Frances visited the stables and came to admire the soft-spoken Josef. Unlike the other brash cowboys, Josef quietly went about his work efficiently taming, and befriending, both stallions and mares alike. She noticed a quiet assurance about him when he gently calmed a frightened gelding, much as she would have done if she were in his place. His strength and kindness were evident in every task he undertook. Josef himself was smitten every time he saw Vincent's only child and soon regularly spoke with her after Sunday services. By the time that winter settled into the country, with Vincent's and Frances' approval, Josef began actively courting the beguiling daughter of his boss.

Christmas that year was particularly joyous as the Riskes celebrated their good fortune, and welcomed Suzanna's newest daughter, Franciszka, into their family on January 28, 1876. She was a happy, beautiful girl that brought sweetness and laughter to all at her newborn antics.

When confronted with his options as his cousins began planning to return to Dakota Territory in May when the harsh winter weather began to break, Josef decided to stay in Winona again. As enticing as they made Dakota Territory sound, he found he wasn't yet ready to leave the treasures he had unearthed in Winona.

Visions Revealed

When the cousins reached Grand Forks with their recently purchased mules and ox, they went to the registrar's office and declared their intention to naturalize—to become citizens of America. After a period of 5 years of continuous residence in the country, with no history of criminal offenses, immigrants could obtain citizenship by paying a two-dollar fee, which the Riske cousins did.

After celebrating their new status at a local saloon, they met with Flying Goose to hire him to help them continue to break their vast holdings. Upon reaching their property, their labor continued steadily as the land slowly awakened from its winter rest. Hundreds of goslings waddled behind their long-necked mothers beneath the endless sky. Black bears awakened from their burrows while bobcats harried newborns for an easy meal. Shooting stars danced in the skies as fireflies twinkled just beyond their evening campfire.

After almost two months of sunup to sundown non-stop work, the cousins were becoming concerned when they noticed large groups of Indians traveling just to the north of their property. Flying Goose explained that his tribe was going to hold a powwow there when the sun reached its highest position in the sky and invited them to join the festivities. When they learned that this would be the last summer solstice held there, and was similar to the Polish *midsummer* festivals, they agreed to participate in something they might never have the opportunity to see again. It would be a welcome break from their daily labor.

On the day of the powwow, everyone rose at dawn to fully enjoy the longest day of sunlight in the year. The cousins attended with Flying Goose, both for their protection, and as interpreter of the ceremonies.

Each clan of the Chippewa paraded together into the central gathering point until all clans were present: the Bullhead, Crane, Pintail Duck, Bear, and Moose-tail clans. Each clan was bedecked with beaded and dyed images, or the fur, feathers, or claws of their clan mascot. The men wore buckskin pants, vests, bandanas, and headdresses while the women wore grass or buckskin-fringed dresses accentuated with shells, quills, and brightly colored jewelry.

Jan felt that the images he witnessed that day would forever be etched into his memory. They were a people proud of their heritage, yet exuberant and filled with joy throughout the festivities. Male and female dancers joined the beating of the drums and the songs, participating whenever they felt moved to do so. Children played and demonstrated their newly developed skills. It was an exciting, wild, invigorating display of an entirely foreign culture, and he thrilled at the sight of it. He questioned Flying Goose about a large, elaborately pictoform-decorated lodge—one that many men entered, but was tightly sealed after they entered.

Flying Goose amiably explained, "That is our vision and dream quest lodge. In there, water is poured over hot rocks to produce steam, and all of the entrances are closed, to enhance the occurrence of dreams and visions for those fasting. Sometimes we add pine or birch bows to the rocks to cause the participants to sweat and heal. The experience cleanses those who enter so that they may attain contact with the beyond.

"We believe the spirit world informs and guides the material world. Each clan has an official dreamer, a visionary, who is skilled at accessing important dreams or visions. They often see the future and tell us where we will find food, or may warn us of trials we may face.

"We have learned that fasting helps one's ability to access this knowledge, so we reduce our intake of food when we seek spiritual guidance. Most adults are able to interpret what they see, but since children are unskilled in the art, we weave dream-catchers and place them over the children as they sleep so that they won't be disturbed by things they don't understand.

"Over there," he said, pointing to a particularly large lodge, "is where our priests and priestesses meet to share their acquired wisdom. There will be a Great Medicine Dance during this powwow where the sacred drum and pipe will be used to initiate new healers into their chosen profession. They will be given medicine bags that contain objects of their specialty: things like glass beads, sacred shells, or carved figures. The most skillful will be allowed to study our ancient stories that have been recorded on birch bark."

Jan nodded at Flying Goose's explanations and said, "We pay little heed to dreams, but if they work, I could certainly use one of those dream-catchers for my wife. She suffers from nightmares from time to time."

Flying Goose was saddened that his new friends were so ignorant of the spiritual world and the guidance it could provide them. He decided then and there that he would craft a dream-catcher to trap their dreams, and would place one above each of their bunks. He knew without doubt that dreams were important to remember, and that they would benefit if they learned how to interpret and use them in their lives. At the very least, the gifts could trap their nightmares before they could create havoc in their daily interactions.

After much feasting, story-telling, trading, and physical skill contests, at the conclusion of the powwow, the tribes were informed of the visions received by the primary dreamer. He declared that his spirit guides revealed that their greatest enemy, the Sioux, would no longer be a threat to the Chippewa nation. Great rejoicing accompanied this news and the clans disbursed, relieved and happier than when they had first gathered.

Several days later they learned about the Battle of the Little Bighorn, or as the Chippewa called it, the Battle of the Greasy Grass, where the Sioux had defeated the American 7th Cavalry. General George Custer was killed, as were 268 other soldiers, with 55 others injured.

After their conquest, the victorious Sioux Indians moved to Canada to avoid retaliation by the American government. That December near Fort Benton, 5,000 Sioux met with Canadian Mountie Commander Walsh, who laid down the rules for their living in Canada: there would be no fighting, no raids against Indians or whites, and no traveling into American territory. The mighty Sioux were no longer a direct threat to the Dakota settlers or the Chippewa nation.

Commuting

For the rest of that summer the four men planted what they could and continued to break the soil for further planting the next year. After downing a buffalo and trapping a beaver, Flying Goose introduced the Riskes to the delicacies of buffalo tongue and beaver's tail. They were never without sustenance as their aim improved with the flocks of geese, cranes and ducks that permeated the area.

The men set up trap-lines that yielded beaver fur, which could be sold for the making of felt hats—which no respectable man would be without—in addition to wildcat, wolverine, and rabbit fur. Beaver pelts were selling for $3.50 per pound, and lynx and wolverine pelts for $2.40 each. The hare fur and goose down was saved for comforter and pillow filler. They even collected buffalo bones on their property that could be sold for fertilizer. They also plotted where they would place their cabins and turned the soil for gardens for the next year. The cabin sites they selected would provide both sunlight and drainage, and were placed in locations best suited to manage the farms. It was a busy, productive summer and they returned to Winona for the winter completely satisfied with their progress.

Suzanna had been busy with her job and their two daughters. Each time Jan returned to his wife's arms, she became pregnant once again. Over the winter of 1877 Jan prayed that this next child would be a boy: he needed sons to help him build their homestead. Just before he left for Dakota on April 15, 1878, Suzanna presented him with his third daughter, Anastasia. Although disappointed she wasn't male, he embraced his new offspring with the love she deserved and marveled at the perfection bequeathed to them from the Lord.

This year Jan vowed to spend the winter on his own property. He wanted to be certain he and his family could survive the elements. After breaking and planting more land when he arrived, he planted potatoes, corn, beets, cucumbers, and cabbage. He would make pickles with the cucumbers and sauerkraut with the cabbage. The potatoes and beets would overwinter well in either the cabin or the root cellar he was hoping to dig.

His work at the lumber mill had taught him the skills necessary to fell and prepare timber for housing. At the west end of his property there was several stands of pine, elm, and birch trees. He would start with a rough, 14 by 14 foot single room cabin with a fireplace, and if he had time, a root cellar to store the produce he would need to survive the winter.

Jan chose straight, old-growth trees with few limbs or knots, so they would not need to be hewn to fit well together. He felled the trees he would need, trimmed them of their branches, and used his mule to drag each one to the site he had chosen. After removing brush and leveling the ground from the planned location, he placed large stones where the cabin corners and the door threshold would be. With the help of Flying Goose, they carefully notched the logs to minimize the size of the gap between them to reduce the amount of mud or corn cobs needed to fill any openings. They then interlocked the rough logs one upon the other until the walls were built.

They also placed supporting beams atop the breadth of the walls to construct and support the slanted roof it would need to enable the winter snow's weight, once accumulated, to fall to the ground and relieve the pressure on the cabin's ceiling.

The cabin roof was constructed with a rafter where the logs were progressively shortened to form a triangular gabled top. The half-hewn roof logs were covered with long, hand-split shingles on which Jan worked during the evenings. They built a stone-lined fireplace and a rough-hewn log floor, flat side up, above the damp soil to allow for a root cellar beneath the cabin. Jan wanted easy access to that during the long winter months ahead.

Later when Jan built their larger house, he would convert this cabin to a chicken coop or tool shed. They also put together a rough lean-to shelter and water trough for their mules and ox to be able to weather the worst of the winter elements.

Julius had chosen to turn more soil and plant more fields rather than build his own cabin since the dugout was on his side of the Forrest River. With no wife or children to be concerned about Frank was in no hurry to build his cabin, but did start felling trees and moving them to his property. He and Flying Goose did that while Jan chinked his cabin and dug his storage cellar.

After harvesting their crops and gathering their produce, they all abided by God's edict in Genesis 1:29–"Behold, I have given you every plant yielding seed that is on the surface of all the earth, and every tree which has fruit yielding seed; it shall be food for you"—and prepared their seed for the next year.

The men had followed the age-old custom of not planting all of their seeds from their original packages in the event their first year's planting didn't succeed because of late frosts which could require them to plant again. They used the most attractive and productive plants in their gardens for seeds: those that bore large fruit, had good flavor, and were resistant to disease. They saved these seeds from at least three different plants to provide pollination for future plantings.

They dried the seeds they wanted to keep in Jan's cabin and the dugout before they stored them. Individual seeds were separated from one another so that they could dry more evenly. They knew that generally the drier the seed, the longer the seed would remain alive in a cloth bag in a dry, cool area such as Jan's cabin or the storage cellar.

When their chores were done for the season, Julius and Frank both had work obligations so were returning to Winona. Jan accompanied them to Grand Forks taking their yields and selling them there; then he gathered the tea, coffee, ammunition, and other necessities he would need for the winter. He promised to care for their mule and ox while they were gone, and wished them a safe journey, sending his love, and several corncob dolls and a dream-catcher from Flying Goose, to his family.

The day after they left the first thing Jan did was travel about 6 miles west of his homestead. Flying Goose had told him there was a forest in that region where he could gather firewood for the winter. He took both mules, his ax, saw and rope, and headed in that direction.

A shallow creek ran north across the property where the forest stood. He cut down several trees in the chilly weather and hauled them back to his cabin. It hadn't snowed yet, but the temperature was dropping so he continued his labor for several days until he felt he had enough timber to make it through the winter. On his last trip, he noticed that there didn't appear to be a land claim in that area.

Owning that forest beside the creek, with flat ground to the south and east of it, would give him the timber he would need to build a proper house to hold his growing family, and he could plant orchards there to supplement his income. Excited at the prospect, he walked the area and staked the corners of the land he wanted. The very next day he traveled to Grand Forks and placed a tree claim for the property. *God had surely blessed him.* Now all he had to do was survive the winter.

The Neighbors

Each day he chopped firewood until he had piles of it surrounding the animal lean-to within easy walking distance from the cabin. He spent his spare daylight hours hunting, setting up a new trap line on his tree claim, enduring the bitingly cold temperatures, but marveling at the shimmering countryside surrounding him.

The first gentle snowfall had covered the ground, leaving a thin mantel of white over everything, except the dark tree trunks. The black and white contrast with the slightly overcast skies, presented stunning silhouettes that inflamed Jan's soul with admiration. One grove of pine trees looked like they were decorated with bright white solid clouds suspended on their branches. When the weather warmed up several days later, he awoke to a vision of every visible branch and twig etched in sunlit ice. For Jan, the glory of nature in sleep was one of God's greatest gifts.

One day while on a hunting and trapping sojourn, Jan met a Norwegian gentleman with a homestead to the north of Frank's, who when he learned Jan was spending the winter there, invited him for Christmas dinner. Although neither could speak the others' language, their English was good enough for the invitation to be understood and graciously accepted—if the weather permitted travel.

Jan left him with a smile on his face. Mr. Anderson was amazing! Much like him he was friendly, independent, and courageous enough to be living on the edges of the wilderness—despite the rigors of Dakota weather.

By the time Christmas arrived, although he had been busy stretching and tanning the hides his trap line had snared, Jan was ready for some human company. He made the several mile journey without too much difficulty, even though the snow was deep, his handmade snowshoes easily allowed him to reach his Norwegian neighbors. The Andersons lived in a turf-house, evidently similar to those built in Norway, with several sheep and a horse in a similar sod-block building.

When he arrived, two attentive sheep-dogs loudly announced his approach. Jan was welcomed with wide smiles and enticing aromas as the Anderson's invited him into their home. He could tell they were both industrious by the fur rugs scattered around the room, the dried herbs hanging from the ceiling, and a spinning wheel with baskets of wool waiting to be processed. Looking at their modest but well-supplied homestead, he felt they had reason to be proud of the accomplishments they were making on the frontier.

Mrs. Anderson bustled around, adding finishing touches to the meal. She had outdone herself by serving *lutefisk* (a lye-treated fish), *knoephla* (a thick, stew-like chicken dumpling soup) and *fleischkuekle* (a deep fried entrée of ground deer meat covered in dough). She served *lefsa* (flat bread made from riced potatoes coated with butter and sugar), *kuchen* (a chokecherry filled pastry), and a cinnamon and apple *strudel* pastry for dessert.

Mrs. Anderson didn't say much other than encouraging him to eat more and refilling his mug with coffee. Jan relished the feast and lavishly complimented Mrs. Anderson's culinary talents.

Mr. Anderson nodded while rubbing his stomach and said, "*Jah*, my wife, she good cook. *Uf-dah*. I, too, am full."

While sitting by the blazing fire, Mr. Anderson indicated with gestures and broken English that they had learned of Dakota Territory through a newspaper advertisement, and traveled to and through Canada to reach this land. They all burst into laughter at times when hand gestures and words were not comprehended, but faces were puzzled with confusion. When a thought was finally understood, they grinned good-naturedly at their accomplishment, saying "ah, ah, ah."

Jan learned that the Andersons had dreams of breeding a sheep herd to supply the area with wool and Mr. Anderson showed Jan the loom he was constructing for his wife. Jan was impressed with the couple's industriousness, thinking they should do well given their apparent energy.

The Eagle's Nest

When it was time to leave, a north wind had picked up and the beginnings of a blizzard was in progress, so Mr. Anderson offered to return Jan home using his horse-drawn sled. The journey went quickly with the wind pushing at their backs, and when Jan mentioned he was running low on firewood, Mr. Anderson offered to help him cart more timber with his sleigh. Jan gratefully accepted his offer, thanked him profusely for his kindness, and told him he would be ready whenever the weather cleared.

After saying their goodbyes, Jan celebrated his good fortune with a nip of a cherished bottle of vodka, and later welcomed the New Year of 1879 with readings of his favorite Bible passages. He felt truly blessed.

❦

In February when the snow was still deep and the pale sun could not warm the frigid air, Jan was surprised to hear a knock on his door in the early afternoon. Wondering if he imagined it, he hurried over to open it, gun in hand. Standing outside was a sopping wet gentleman, shivering with cold.

"Come in, come in," Jan immediately said, grabbing his arm and pulling him into the cabin. "What happened?"

"I was trying to cross the river when I misjudged the depth of the ice and it gave way, and my horse and I both got soaked," the stranger explained.

"Please, please, come in and sit by the fire," Jan hurriedly said, pointing him to a short tree stump beside the hearth, "before you breathe your last breath."

"Thank you. I'm Doctor Wilson," he said, shaking Jan's hand. "I was just returning from delivering a baby a couple of miles north of here when it happened. I'm afraid I *will* catch my death if I try to continue to Grand Forks in these wet things. Do you have an extra set of clothing you could loan me, so I can make it home tonight? I'll be happy to return them to you as soon as I can."

"My name is Jan Riske, I'm pleased to meet you. I'm sorry about your accident. Are you injured at all?"

"No, no, just a few bruises, other than being nearly frozen to death. I don't think I have frostbite yet. I'll be on my way quickly, if you can help me out."

Mary Barton

"I'm sorry," Jan shook his head in embarrassment, "I only have the clothes I am wearing and an extra pair of socks. But we can get you out of those wet things and wrap you in a quilt while your clothes dry out. Change over there by my pallet and take the blanket to cover yourself while I build up the fire. There's a towel near the water bucket to dry yourself off."

Dr. Wilson nodded in astonishment as he glanced around the snug but bare cabin, where one corner was filled with a variety of animal hides. As cold as he was, it didn't take him long to follow Jan's instructions, but now he was chagrined by his request.

He was an educated man, who could speak English, German and French, and had been enchanted by Dakota Territory after serving with his brother in a military fort to the west of there. After they ended their service, they settled in Grand Forks, enticed to do so by the city's need for a doctor, and his desire to watch out for his adventurous younger brother who recognized the business opportunities of the area. As a medical doctor, he made a decent living, and had more clothes than he needed, yet here he was at the mercy of a kind immigrant who was saving his life without thinking twice about it.

Jan placed more logs on the fire, took Dr. Wilson's wet clothes and threw them over the line he had stretched to dry his own clothes when he washed them. His other set of clothes had been ruined at the coal mine, and he had never replaced them, as all his extra funds went toward supplying the homestead.

Unhappy that he couldn't provide the doctor with what he needed, he immediately set about offering him what he could by brewing coffee and adding more meat and vegetables to the stew pot. He then went outside, rubbed down the doctor's horse, and made sure it had food and shelter. When he returned inside, he sat down on a mountain lion skin not far from the fire himself.

"Babies can come at some of the worst times," Dr. Wilson commented, as his body temperature began to return to normal beneath the warm quilt. "That's some lion skin you've got there. Did you down that yourself?"

Jan smiled in pleasure at the memory, slowly answering, "Yes," he admitted, "I got my coat rack at the same time," nodding to a pair of elk antlers mounted on a wall. "One day I came across a herd of foraging elk that seemed unnaturally restless. I watched them for a while until I saw what was making them nervous. There was this mountain lion slowly creeping up on the herd. When the mountain lion leaped and downed one of them with a direct throat kill, I sighted on the lion and brought it down. Best kill I ever made."

Dr. Wilson laughed at Jan's triumph, "Well, that was good luck."

Jan nodded at the stew pot and said, "Yes, and I'm still enjoying the elk. I was just fortunate the smell of the blood didn't alert any other predators before I made it home. My mule was real skittish packing them back."

They exchanged pleasantries and their stories over dinner until the clothes were deemed dry enough to wear. After a heartfelt thank you from Dr. Wilson, he headed towards home on a route Jan recommended where the river was frozen enough to cross safely. Jan had enjoyed the company and was satisfied that he had made a new friend.

After the visit, Jan borrowed Mr. Anderson's sled to haul more timber from his tree claim to build a bunk bed, table, and a couple of benches for the cabin, to be better able to entertain guests when they dropped by. He also wanted to start the construction of a wagon. Their yields were becoming large enough that a wagon would be a big help carting their produce to market.

Several weeks later at the beginning of March, Jan asked Flying Goose to watch his property and check his trap lines for him while he was gone. He would pay him for doing so with one-half of any pelts and all the meat he collected from his traps. He wanted to return to Winona for a spell to see his family and replenish his depleted money. Tree saplings would also need to be purchased to start his 40 acre orchard. He wanted to begin improving that property this spring so that he wouldn't lose it. It was a prime blessing he meant to keep.

Renewed Hope

Suzanna was grateful for her work at the grist mill, knowing that her meager earnings would help their family accomplish their goals. She regularly attended church, observing it's many Holy Days, and prayed daily for Jan's safety. She worried about him being out in the wilderness on his own, and hoped he hadn't taken ill, or been scalped by some renegade Indian. Julius had assured her when he returned that Jan had ample food and the cabin was a stout one that should shelter him from the freezing temperatures.

She pulled out her Bible to remind herself from Philippians 4:6-8: "Do not be anxious about anything, but in everything by prayer and supplication with thanksgiving let your requests be made known to God. And the peace of God, which surpasses all understanding, will guard your hearts and your minds in Christ Jesus. Finally, brothers, whatever is true, whatever is honorable, whatever is just, whatever is pure, whatever is lovely, whatever is commendable, if there is any excellence, if there is anything worthy of praise, think about these things." She finally decided to distract herself by concentrating on each blessing she had received and to trust in God, rather than make herself ill with worry.

Her children were a constant delight to her. The girls were sprouting up as fast as wisteria, blossoming and reaching out to, and attaching themselves whole-heartedly to new areas of growth. They were learning English quickly from Martin's children, as well as the Polish she spoke to them. All four of them slept in the same bed in a room in Martin's house, and she helped with the household chores, although Martin's older children hauled water, and kept the firewood box full. In her spare time she knit socks, mittens, scarves, and shawls for the family. She did miss her husband's company but was becoming accustomed to her life as an independent female.

The freedom to do as she pleased was invigorating, and she was amazed at the change in herself since coming to America. Where once she had been shy, being forced to work had challenged her to become more outgoing with strangers, and given the opportunity, to readily make friends with both sexes. But she was sorry Jan wasn't there to treasure their children's unique personalities and achievements.

In the evenings she tried to make up for his absence by telling them stories of his adventures to remind them that they did indeed have a father who loved them. Josef frequently entertained them, too, and they had come to love him and blossomed under his playful attentiveness. This was the first year she wasn't pregnant since her marriage and her figure had returned to its natural gracefulness, and many admiring male eyes turned her way when she walked to work. She secretly enjoyed the attention, but never encouraged any overtures.

She was chatting with a male co-worker when she left her job one day in mid-March, laughing about some comment he had made when she saw a man she thought she recognized standing outside in the warehouse yard. Thinking she was imagining things, as the man had long hair and a full beard, she bid the coworker a good evening with a bright smile and continued on her way.

Jan watched their exchange with consternation, then approached her saying, "Surely you have a better welcome for your husband?"

"Jan? Jan! You're back!" she exclaimed as they embraced awkwardly in the street. She wasn't expecting him, and felt distanced from him and unprepared for his return.

"You should have told me you were coming!" she scolded, as she pulled back and she gazed at his new appearance. "You let your hair grow!"

"I wanted to surprise you," he said with a look toward the receding man, "and evidently I did. Who was that you were talking to?"

"Oh, that was Samuel, just one of the men I work with," she replied, surprisingly irritated by his question. She had forgotten about his tendency toward jealousy, and reasoned that he had been the one to leave her, and their children, to fend for themselves. But this was her husband and it was her duty to become reacquainted with the father of her children. "He's from Warsaw," she finally settled on saying nonchalantly. "We often chat about what is happening in Poland. He's working here until he can return home."

Jan didn't recognize anything but an innocent response on her face when she replied, so he let the subject drop, but took her arm as they turned toward home. He despised the fact that she had to work at all—but it was common for the poor to do so and they sincerely needed the money. How he wished he was rich and could keep her in a style that she deserved. His inadequacy to completely provide for his family wounded his ego, but he knew he was trying as hard as he could to do just that, and soon he hoped to accomplish that goal.

"You are looking lovelier than ever," he said, keeping his misgivings to himself.

"Oh, Jan, I'm sure I look frightful after a full day of work!" she replied self-consciously, as she checked that her hair was completely covered by her *babushka*. Boldly reaching over and stroking his beard she added, "This may take some getting used to."

He nodded at her, finally with a smile, at her show of playfulness, "My beard helped keep my face from getting frost-bitten in the freezing temperatures while I did my chores. It gets as cold there as it does in Poland in the winter. Come, let's get home. I have so much to tell you. How are our daughters?"

"Healthy, missing their father as much as I do."

He was relieved by her reply. *She did miss him.* And he *had* missed his family and was happy to be rejoined with them. He pulled her closer to him and wrapped his arms around her shoulders as they hurried along.

"Well, we'll soon rectify that," he said affectionately.

"Why did you come back early?"

"I wanted to spend Easter with you and the children. I did miss you, you know. I also needed to purchase what I need for the farm. The stores are so expensive there with their limited stock and slow turnover, that I thought it would be better to purchase items here where prices are more reasonable. I could negotiate prices with the store owners, but I don't want to deal on credit based on our future crops. It's better for me to return here and earn the money we will need to supply the farm. Flying Goose is taking care of the stock for me but I need to discuss a few options with Julius and Frank."

She nodded at his response, but didn't mention her misgivings at how he could be friends with an Indian when one had brutally killed Victor. All of the men admired the half-breed: she just didn't understand it. She still had the continuing nightmare of a savage standing over her body, no matter how often she prayed for God to dispel it. Unknown to Jan, she had quietly discarded the heathen dream-catcher Flying Goose had sent her with repulsion. Dispelling the unbidden thoughts from her mind, she asked instead, "Did you miss me?"

"As if my heart had been torn from my chest," he responded, stroking her cheek with his hand.

Suzanna was gratified by his reply: he did love her. It would take some getting used to having him back again after almost a year's absence, but she must try hard for her children's sake.

When they reached home, everyone was excited by Jan's news of his tree claim. That could indeed be a money-making proposition.

"Yes," Jan agreed, "I think it can. One day I used a neighbor's sled and hauled several trees to the lumber mill. I traded a couple of furs I trapped for them to plane some flat boards for me to build a wagon base, and purchased the wheels at a newly-opened blacksmith shop. I now own a wagon!"

Everyone, including Suzanna, was impressed by his industry, his hunting successes, and the stories of his encounters with their neighbors. Maybe things would work out to their advantage for a change.

"The town is really growing fast," he continued. "There are at least 1,000 people living in the city now. They even built a Presbyterian Church and have started building wood plank sidewalks in the business district. I think we should consider moving there permanently next year after we get your cabins built this summer. I don't want to lose our property to any claim-jumpers."

Since Jan's wintering had been successful, although he did tell of several fierce blizzards and high snowdrifts he had to deal with for months, they all agreed it was probably a sound idea. They would start preparing what they would need to move and survive there permanently.

Jan returned to the lumber mill working long hours, but also found time to cherish the evenings spent with his delightful daughters. He good-naturedly teased, loved, and developed a mutually devoted bond with each of them. His efforts were rewarded when they ran to him and vied for his attention at the end of the day excitedly sharing their accomplishments with him. He also renewed his intimacy with his wife with a vengeance and revealed the wonders of their property and his plans for their future with her. When spring convinced the trees and bushes to flower and bear fruit, they discovered that Suzanna would be doing the same as another addition to the family was in production.

Josef, meanwhile, found that he liked Winona. The bustling riverboat community brought hundreds of travelers seeking their fortunes daily to the local piers. His grasp of the English, German and Polish languages enabled him to communicate with most of them to learn the different aspects of other parts of this nation. He enjoyed interacting with those who visited the stables to purchase the horses they would need to continue their journeys.

Josef was still courting Vincent's daughter and as his cousins made their plans to return to the west, he was reluctant to leave. With his knowledge of horseflesh, he had become an integral part of Vincent's business, allowing the older man some long deserved rest from running the lucrative business. Although trains were becoming more common for long journeys, horses were still in high demand, and once he had the necessary capital, he was considering opening his own breeding business.

His reputation as an exceptional horse trainer was becoming known in the city, and those folks who purchased from Vincent's stables were spreading the word about the quality of his work. When people learned of his experiences with the Pennsylvania militia, and his having emerged unscathed from one of the largest coal mine disasters in the nation, he was viewed as a man to be respected. Personally, he knew that he now valued life more than he ever had and was determined to enjoy the blessings given him.

He had discovered a prime piece of property that was for sale, and as his feelings grew for Frances, he was putting more money away with the hopes of winning her heart and having the funds to provide a home for her. He found he couldn't consider leaving Frances nor his beloved job to move to Dakota Territory. For now, he decided to once again stay in Winona when his cousins went west.

The Eagle's Nest

Although Jan's stay in Winona had been a short one, the men left soon after the weather warmed to tend to their homesteads. They quickly planted their crops, and Julius decided he would be content with the dugout for his wife and two toddlers, and would build his cabin the following year. He wanted to clear more land as he would need good yields to provide for his family without any guaranteed additional income. Frank did put up a small cabin with attached quarters for his mule and any additional livestock he would purchase.

Using Suzanna's earnings, Jan bought twenty apple tree saplings that he had brought with him. He hauled them to the tree property using his newly constructed wagon, planted them, and spent several warm spring days further investigating the forest. There were plenty of trees that would be ideal for building both a barn and a larger dwelling for his growing family. Given a good harvest, he could probably afford to have the trees milled there for constructing them the next year. Until then, given his growing family, he added a loft for the girls to sleep in, and shelving for Suzanna's kitchen utensils.

The days passed quickly with their continuous, non-stop labor. Clearing brush by hand, furrowing with their single plow each, planting, and harvesting acres primarily by hand was a slow process, but the weather favored them and their harvests had been profitable. When they returned in the fall, Flying Goose again agreed to watch their places, and would meet them in Grand Forks with the wagon in the spring to haul their household goods to their properties. They all returned to Winona for the winter to earn the money they would need to bring their families to Dakota Territory.

On a cold blustery day, January 18, 1880, Suzanna presented Jan with Paulina, his fourth daughter. Disappointed the newborn was yet another girl, he did welcome his new daughter and knew he would cherish her as much as he did each of his children.

With her father's consent, Josef had asked Frances to marry him at Christmas. She had blessedly agreed and a spring wedding was planned so everyone would be able to attend before they left to live permanently in Dakota Territory.

Blessed Unions

*J*osef nervously paced the church sanctuary. He hoped he wasn't making a grievous mistake. Memories of Little Turtle rejecting him kept surfacing in his mind as he waited for the organ music to announce the beginning of his thoroughly American wedding ceremony. *Had he made the right decision to marry Frances and buy property in Winona? What if he was wrong and Frances was as capricious as Little Turtle had been? Could she really love a simple Pole such as himself? He didn't know if he could survive the heartbreak if Frances had a hidden fickle nature.*

As the time for the beginning of the ceremony had passed and the music still hadn't begun yet, doubts flooded into his mind. *Had he been duped and was about to be played the fool?*

Second-guessing his decisions, thoughts of Jan and Suzanna and their daughters living so far from him entered his mind. Jan was like a brother to him, and Suzanna, a sister. He would miss them tremendously, they had been through so much together. And he *adored* Jan and Suzanna's cherubs, having practically become their surrogate father when Jan was away during the past couple of years. As the time drew closer to their departure, he knew he would miss watching them grow into womanhood. *Should he have settled in Dakota Territory instead of deciding to stay in Winona?*

The anxiety displayed on Josef's face made his best man, Jan, laugh and pull a flask of vodka from his pocket.

"Here," he said to Josef. "Have a sip. It will settle your nerves."

"Where is she?" Josef asked anxiously. "What if she changed her mind?"

"She didn't change her mind, Josef," Jan replied firmly with a shake of his head. "You know women. They are never on time for anything. She is just running late. She probably snagged her stockings and needed to find a replacement, or her hair wasn't to her liking and she had to rearrange it. She'll be here. How could she leave a man like you at the altar? You two were meant for each other! She knows she will never find another man who doesn't care whether she is as good with horses as he is."

Josef laughed, as he took a quick drink. Jan was right. The woman could gentle a frightened horse as well as any man. He had seen her do it. They had so much in common, and she had been thrilled with the ranch he had purchased, and his plans to start a horse breeding business. She *seemed* to be excited at the thought of their eminent union, so where was she? She had been terribly secretive lately, rushing about on unexplained errands, refusing to reveal what she was up to. Would he *ever* understand women?

At that moment, the organist began playing the wedding march. Releasing a sigh of relief, he handed the flask back to Jan, who tucked it in his pocket, and together they stepped through the door and onto the steps of the altar. When Josef looked to the back of the church, he was gratified to see it was filled with the many friends he had made since arriving in Winona. He also saw his Uncle Martin and his extended family as well as Frances' relatives, all there to bear witness to their union.

He then smiled broadly as he watched Mary, Franciszka, and Anastasia rapidly scamper down the aisle, tossing flower petals from their beribboned baskets. Suzanna followed close behind with a pink rose bouquet in hand, dressed in a delicate floral print dress in the same fabric as that of her daughter's gowns. Josef had been so pleased when in honor of their long association, and the recent budding friendship between them, Frances had asked Suzanna to be her matron of honor. She looked captivating as ever.

Once they were all settled in their positions at the front of the church, the organist's music riveted everyone's eyes to the back of the church where Frances appeared, resplendent in her wedding dress, a timorous smile on her face. Josef's breath caught in his throat at the sight of her, a rush of desire animating his body.

Vincent was on her left side, a proud grin on his face as he started to guide his beloved daughter down the church aisle. Just as took their first step, another man joined them on Frances' right side, with a look of mischief on his face.

Josef's mouth dropped open in shock. *He must be seeing things. It couldn't be!*

But it was. Josef's younger brother strode determinedly down the short aisle beside Frances. Tears streamed down Josef's face at the joy of seeing a member of his immediate family, one whom he had thought to never see again. Josef couldn't have been more surprised or overcome with emotion then he was at that moment. When they reached the front of the church, he rushed to firmly embrace his brother, kissing his face repeatedly as tears streamed down his own.

Long moments later, wiping the tears from his face with his handkerchief, he patted his brother on the back and turned to where Frances and Vincent were waiting with triumph on their faces. Vincent placed Frances' hand in Josef's and said, "I know you will take good care of my daughter. You are like the son I never had but now do. Welcome to the family, Josef."

Josef nodded, firmly shaking Vincent's hand, not trusting himself to speak being once again overcome with emotion at Vincent's words.

As her father stepped away to his seat, Frances murmured quickly to Josef, "Your brother is my wedding gift to you. I want you to be happy here, Josef. I know it was a difficult decision for you to make to stay in Winona and not seek your fortune in Dakota Territory, but I am so incredibly thankful that you did. With Jan and Suzanna leaving, I didn't want you to feel lonely. I know how much your family means to you. All of your stories of what you and your brother did together when you were younger, inspired me to bring you together again. Suzanna was kind enough to help me arrange it. I love you so much, Josef. Your love and happiness mean the world to me. Are you pleased with my present?"

Josef looked at his bride in wonder. Not only was she beautiful but she was kind-hearted enough to honestly care about his complete well-being. How could he ever have doubted her sincerity? Lovingly gazing into her eyes, he said, "You are the most cherished gift I have ever received, my love. Shall we pledge ourselves to each other?" he asked as he motioned them forward to where the priest awaited them.

The ceremony went quickly and soon they were celebrating their new roles as husband and wife. "How did you manage to bring my brother over here?" he asked his wife.

"It wasn't easy," Frances responded with a sigh. "But with Suzanna's help we were able to get Father Ignacio to spirit him out of the country in Poland, and my father to meet him in New York."

"Your father?"

"Yes, that trip he supposedly made to escort my aunt here for the wedding, was actually when he went to meet your brother. As a business owner, he was able to sponsor him and guarantee him a job. It all worked out rather well. Although, my father swears he will never step foot in New York again! The crowds there made him yearn to be back in more open country."

Jan shook his head at the good-heartedness of his new family. How would he ever repay them for the joy they had brought into his life? He was so thoroughly blessed, he knew he would never stop trying.

Paradise Found

Jan and Suzanna smiled as they watched Mary and Franciszka play cat's cradle. Anastasia clung to her father in fright at their strange surroundings while Suzanna suckled Paulina. Mary was 6 years old, Franciszka 4, Anastasia 2, and Paulina barely 4-months-old. They didn't have much household goods, but Julius and Frank did, so they had decided to rent an entire train boxcar to hold the three families and their property. Suzanna had her trunks they had brought from Poland, the cradle Jan had made, and a farewell gift of a handmade rocker from Uncle Martin.

Having lived in America for most of their lives, Julius and Frank had two bed frames, two water basins, a vanity and mirror, three rocking chairs, and farming tools in addition to kitchen implements. All of which was piled in the wagon their father had given them, and had been driven into the boxcar with them. There were baskets filled with linens, pillows and quilts. The group also brought along a couple of pigs, a pregnant sow, two more mules, another ox, and laying hens and roosters in pens.

As the pioneers sat on the bags of oats, wheat and vegetable seeds they had brought along, the trip went fairly quickly with tending to the children and eating from baskets of prepared bread, cheese, and dried fruits. Three casks of fresh water, which they refilled at every stop they made, sated the thirst of all the living creatures. They spent their spare time playing card games, doing needlework, or discussing their plans for when they arrived. The men, in particular, were discussing building barns, chicken and pig pens, and considering later preparing ice houses to keep their game frozen, and to have ice for cold drinks and making ice cream in the summer.

When they arrived at Fisher's Landing, they loaded Jan's wagon Flying Goose had brought with their goods and the family members to carry them to their destination. Suzanna kept her distance from Flying Goose but surreptitiously observed him, and noted that he was a fairly young man with a ready smile that he sent to each of the new family members. As Suzanna couldn't speak much English, she merely nodded to him at his greeting. The trip took longer than previous ones, despite the help of the additional mules and ox, as each wagon was filled to capacity.

When they reached the ferry station, they saw that it was no longer in operation but had been replaced by a pontoon toll bridge that charged fifteen cents for a horse and rider, and twenty-five cents for a team and wagon. Each wagon was ferried across individually and all were relieved that there were no mishaps. Once on land they headed towards town to give the wives a quick tour of the city.

The village had rapidly grown to about 1,700 residents, and now boasted a Presbyterian Church at the corner of Fifth Street and Belmont, and a new Episcopal Church. The women were delighted to find a Roman Catholic Church built at Third and DeMers street. Although it was 35 miles to their property, they would be able to attend mass and receive the Holy Sacraments at least at Christmas or Easter!

Suzanna smiled broadly at that and was gratified to see the number of stores and the size of the settlement. They wouldn't be too far from civilization. On their way to their cabin, Jan excitedly pointed out the main attractions of the area: herds of deer, flocks of geese, and the Indian encampments to the south of the lake, which Suzanna eyed with both curiosity and suspicion.

When they reached their property, the men proudly displayed their accomplishments to their families. Both women were amazed by the amount of land their husbands had cleared. In the five years that they had been summering there, they each had cultivated almost half of their entire 160 acre plots.

The women were equally happy with the meandering Forrest River. On Jan's section it ran fairly straight, crossing his property from the northeast to the southwest corner, splitting his land in half with flat acreage to either side of it. Near the top end of his property, the river swung east and looped down to the middle of Julius's property then swerved up to the top east end of it. The river then made a crazy zigzag through the east portion of Frank's plot. Each piece of land had fresh, navigable, fish-filled, pure water to sustain them.

Suzanna had to admire Jan's choice of land. It was truly perfect. The plentiful water through his entire land claim guaranteed abundant moisture for all of their crops. They really could live well here. She spontaneously hugged him for his wisdom and the amazing effort he had put in to their property.

For security reasons, and to be better able to easily visit each other, they had built their cabins and dugout near the north end of Julius's and Jan's property, and to the south end of Frank's. That left them not only living close together, near drinking water, but it also left the majority of their acreage free for planting. The Riskes were no fools.

Once she saw it, Amelia was satisfied with their dugout, and knew it would suffice until their cabin could be built. Frank dropped them off with their goods, then continued to his home several acres north of them on the other side of the river, planning to cross at a shallow area he frequently used.

Jan was anxious about Suzanna's reaction to their cabin. After living in Martin's large farmhouse, she might be unhappy at the close living quarters. He had tried his best to make their home comfortable for his family. As he helped his wife down from their wagon, he was relieved when he saw the eagle lift from a nearby tree, circle their property, then fly with out-stretched wings toward the lake. *Praise God,* he thought, *we will find happiness here.*

Jan then confidently hurried to open the door with a sweeping hand to allow his wife to enter first. Suzanna was truly impressed with the amount of work her husband had accomplished. The cabin was well-built, with a stout fireplace, compact but serviceable dining area, and sleeping quarters for her and their young children.

"Oh, Jan," she said as she turned to him, "Thank you so much! It is beautiful!"

Relieved that she liked it, Jan grinned broadly saying, "Only the best for you and our children. You deserve much more, but we will do that in time. I love you with all my heart and think we can really prosper here."

Suzanna embraced him with enthusiasm for what he had done for her. He truly was an outstanding husband. How she had ever doubted him, she didn't know, but she had. Never again would she question his judgment.

She began taking stock of her home immediately. Her home. She could hardly believe it. All of the suffering and agony they had been through had indeed been worth it. Overcome with emotion, she spontaneously dropped down on her knees and thanked God for her husband, and the tremendous gift He had bestowed on their family. Now she understood Jan's excitement. Now she could truly live in peace and pride at who she was and who they were. They were American landowners. Nothing could stop them now.

❧

Glossary

babka: coffeecake in the Polish language
babushka: a headscarf in the Polish language
bramas: gates or portals in the Polish language
chata: a Polish cottage, hut, primitive dwelling, or a place that one lives
czepek: a cap or bonnet in the Polish language
danka: "thank you" in the German language
dummkopf: idiot or fool in the German language
fleischkuekle: a Norwegian deep fried entrée of ground meat covered in dough
Gazeta Narodowa: the "Polish National Gazette" newspaper
ggyen-kuyeh: "thank you" in the Polish language
Gitchie Manitou: the "Supreme Being" in the Chippewa Indian language
gołabki: cabbage rolls, frequently meat filled, in the Polish language.
gorzko: "bitter" in the Polish language
gospodarz: Polish landowners
grosz: Polish monetary denomiation equivalent to approximately one penny
jah: "yes" in the Norwegian language
Kaszub: relating to the Kashubian people and their language from the Pomeranian region of Poland
klepsydra: "funeral notice" in the Polish language
knoephl: a Norwegian thick, stew-like chicken dumpling soup
kuchen: a Norwegian fruit-filled pastry
lefsa: a Norwegian flat bread made from riced potatoes coated with butter and sugar
Les Grandes Fourches: "Grand Forks" in the French language
lokiec: a Polish measurement of one cubit, approximately one foot

lutefisk: a Norwegian lye-treated fish
manoomin: "wild rice" in the Chippewa Indian language
Marzanna: a straw figure representing death, winter, disease and all things considered evil by the Polish people
matka: "mother" in the Polish language
morg: a Polish land measurement approximately equal to one acre
Mozesz pocalowac panne mloda: "you may now kiss the bride" in the Polish language
netap: "friend" in the Lenape Indian language
oberek: a traditional Polish wedding dance
oczepiny: the Polish custom of unveiling the bride
oj: "ah" or "yikes" in the Polish language
ojciec: "father" in the Polish language
oplatek: a Roman Catholic communion wafer in the Polish language
Pączki Day: the Tuesday before Ash Wednesday in the Polish Roman Catholic religion
Philadelphia maneto: "let brotherly love endure" in the Greek language
pierogi: "dumplings" in the Polish language
pogrzeb: "funeral" in the Polish language
Przeglad Polski: the "Polish Review" newspaper
Serdeczna Matko: "Beloved Mother" in the Polish language
strudel: a Norwegian pastry
stypa: a Polish funeral wake
tak: "yes" in the Polish language
topienie Marzanny: "the drowning of Marzanna" in the Polish language
Tung-ul-ung'-si: "Smallest Turtle" in the Lenape Indian language
uf-dah: exclamation in the Norwegian language expressing surprise, astonishment, relief or dismay
We-lung-ung-sil: "Little Turtle" in the Lenape Indian language
wigilia: "Christmas Eve" in the Polish language
Wszędzie dobrze ale w domu najlepiej: "Everywhere is fine but best at home" in the Polish language.

Made in the USA
Middletown, DE
13 December 2019